HOPE FOR
Your
NEW
BEGINNING

WORDS FROM OUR FRIENDS

JERRY FALWELL

"Through David and Barbara Cerullo's leadership, Inspiration Ministries is powerfully spreading the Gospel of Jesus Christ to the world!"

KAY ARTHUR

"I've known David and Barbara Cerullo for years, and I share their passion for sending the uncompromised truth around the world through media."

CHARLES STANLEY

"Multiplied thousands of souls have been won to the Kingdom of Jesus Christ through David Cerullo and Inspiration Ministries. We give God all the glory."

DR. MYLES MUNROE

"What strikes me most about David and Barbara Cerullo is their honesty and humility. Their ministry is worthy of our trust."

JAMES ROBISON

"I believe in David and Barbara Cerullo's leadership. They are seeking to walk in harmony with God's heart, and I believe they're going to win millions of people to Jesus Christ."

RUTH GRAHAM

"David and Barbara Cerullo are powerfully reaching the world with the saving love of Jesus Christ. Their passion to evangelize the nations and the integrity and compassion with which they do this honors the Lord."

DAVID
CERULLO

HOPE FOR

Your

NEW
BEGINNING

Hope for Your New Beginning

by David Cerullo

Copyright © 2006 by David Cerullo

ISBN: 978-1-887600-86-6

Published by

INSPIRATION MINISTRIES

P.O. Box 7750

Charlotte, NC 28241

www.inspiration.org

Printed in the United States of America.

Dedication

I DEDICATE THIS BOOK TO MY
WONDERFUL WIFE, BARBARA,
OUR CHILDREN AND GRANDCHILDREN,
AND OUR INSPIRATION PARTNERS
WHO MAKE IT POSSIBLE TO IMPACT
PEOPLE FOR CHRIST WORLDWIDE
THROUGH MEDIA. AS GOD IS BLESSING
YOU, YOU ARE BLESSING OTHERS,
AND YOUR HEAVENLY REWARD
WILL BE GREAT.

Contents

YOUR SPRINGTIME IS COMING!

THERE ARE ONLY TWO KINDS OF PEOPLE: those who need a New Beginning now and those who will need one soon. No one is exempt. As Jesus told us, the sun and rain are experienced by both the righteous and the unrighteous (Matthew 5:45).

The pages of Scripture are filled with examples of people who received a New Beginning from God. The Lord provides us with these wonderful stories to encourage us by His faithful intervention in the lives of His people, as Paul tells us in Romans 15:4:

> *Whatever was written in earlier times was written for our instruction, so that through perseverance and the encouragement of the Scriptures we might have hope.*

God wants to step into the circumstances of your life today!

THE SEASONS OF LIFE

What season of life are you in right now? Perhaps you are in a stressful season and recognize your need for a New Beginning.

Each of us will face a "winter season" at one time or another. This could be a divorce, an illness, the loss of a loved one, a financial setback, or struggles with our children. When a difficult situation brings *winter* into our life, it's easy to feel frustrated, stressed-out, and overwhelmed.

Even those who have already experienced the *ultimate* new beginning—the New Birth in Jesus Christ (John 3:7)—will periodically find themselves in a difficult spot. Despite being faithful to the Lord, every Believer will, from time to time, need a fresh start…a release from their winter season.

The good news is that a New Beginning is available to anyone who truly wants one. It's not a matter of wishful thinking or just trying harder, and we don't have to be in any doubt about where to find such a breakthrough. Revelation 21:5 tells us: *"He who sits on the throne said, 'Behold, I am making **all** things new.'"*

Perhaps you've been looking for answers to life's questions in all the wrong places: unhealthy friendships, addictions, immorality, binging on food, pornography, or material gain. These may have temporarily distracted you from the real issue, but instead of fixing the ache in your heart, it only grew worse.

However, if you need a New Beginning today, you can be *certain* where to find it: at the throne of Jesus, the One who is able to make ALL things new!

WAITING FOR SPRINGTIME

If you're going through a winter season in your marriage, your job, your health, your finances, or your children…I encourage you to keep on loving, praying, and believing. Sing one more song. Be steadfast and immovable. Pursue, persist, and press on toward the mark of the high calling of God in Christ Jesus. Lay aside every weight holding you down or holding you back. Don't give up until you receive your breakthrough from God.

The more difficult your winter season has been, the deeper your roots can grow in Christ, and the greater your coming harvest will be. And because of the lessons of the winter season, a whole New Beginning can be yours...new joy...new peace...and a new level of contentment in your life in God.

Spring is just around the corner. A spring of greater vision. A spring of answers to prayer.

As you await your springtime, continue trusting in God. Continue crying out to Him. Continue believing His promise to work *ALL* things together for your good (Romans 8:28).

MY PRAYER FOR YOU

My prayer is that you will find new hope and strength from God in the pages of this book. At the end of each chapter, I've included questions to help you apply God's Word to the situations that may be holding you back from your New Beginning. I encourage you to read this book with a Bible and Prayer Journal in hand, ready to ask the Lord for His direction.

You'll get the most out of this book when you follow the psalmist's example of asking God to search your heart:

> *Search me, O God, and know my heart;*
> *Try me and know my anxious thoughts;*
> *And see if there be any hurtful way in me,*
> *And lead me in the everlasting way*
> (Psalm 139:23-24).

Friend, you can be honest with God about any *"hurtful way"* or *"anxious thoughts"* you may be experiencing today. Allow Him to search your heart and lead you in His *"everlasting way"* to your New Beginning.

Remember: Everyone needs a New Beginning some-time—and God offers that New Beginning to YOU *today*! God *IS* faithful! Your springtime *IS* coming!

David

Change is inevitable, and God has a purpose for every season.

GET UNSTUCK FROM *Your* 'WINTER SEASON'

IF YOU ARE GOING THROUGH A DIFFICULT SEASON in your life right now, I want you to know that you can have a New Beginning in Christ today. I don't mean just a momentary touch from God, but rather a lasting divine transformation that enables you to walk victoriously and experience the abundant life Paul describes: *"Thanks be to God, who always leads us in triumph in Christ"* (2 Corinthians 2:14).

However, winter seasons come to each of us from time to time. Sometimes our lives can get so clouded with problems that we even wonder, "Is God there? Does He still care about me? Will He answer my prayers?"

Ecclesiastes 3:1 says, *"To every thing there is a season, a time for every purpose under heaven."* Change is inevitable. Nothing stays the same. There are seasons in our lives. All of life is not summer, and it's not always spring.

Just as every farmer knows, there are times of sowing in the spring. Then in the summer months, he waits for these crops to sprout and grow. When autumn comes, it's time to reap what he's sown. And then there are those cold winter months when everything is dark and dreary, and it seems as though nothing is happening.

Every season is important, and none is more important than the others. It takes time for the seeds we've sown to sprout and turn into crops. Harvests require patience. But the Bible is clear: We *WILL* reap what we sow. Our harvest *WILL* come in due time (Galatians 6:9).

WINTER DOESN'T LAST FOREVER

If you're in a winter season in your life today, you need to realize that it won't last forever. Perhaps you feel like you've been "stuck" in this difficult season for a while now, but God wants to answer your prayers and give you the breakthrough you need.

Regardless of what winter season you're going through, remember these vital truths:

1. There's a reason for the winter seasons in your life.
2. God offers to take you safely through them.
3. He wants to give you a whole New Beginning.

In the natural realm, winter is a stressful season for many of us. Here it's cold and rainy, trees have lost their leaves, and everything seems lifeless. In the winter seasons of our lives, the devil tries to use our circumstances to attack and discourage us.

When we feel the chilly breezes of winter and there are few signs of life around us, Satan will come and whisper, "God doesn't love you or care about you. If He did, He wouldn't have let tragedy strike your life…He wouldn't have let your child get caught up in drugs…He wouldn't have let you get sick…He wouldn't have let you lose your job…or He wouldn't have let your marriage fail."

The devil is a thief, and he plots against us to steal, kill, and destroy—whether physically, financially, relationally, or spiritually. But Jesus said He came that we might have life and have it more abundantly (John 10:10)!

Yet God allows winter experiences to come into our lives, and if we're not careful, these experiences can get us down, depressed, and discouraged. If we focus on our problems and the bigness of our needs, the devil will use our circumstances to bring us frustration and defeat. Instead, we need to look to the bigness of our God and remember His faithfulness, even when it's hard to see signs of it with our natural eyes.

Remember: Although things may look dead in your winter seasons, they're not. When the season changes, spring will surely return, and what appeared dead will come back to life.

But you must be patient. When a winter season strikes your marriage, your job, your children, or your health, you must persistently go to God and ask...seek...and knock (Matthew 7:7). In the original Greek text of this verse, the tense is active and progressive. The literal translation is "ask and keep on asking...seek and keep on seeking...knock and keep on knocking." Perseverance is a key to seeing your prayers answered and a key to coming through your winter seasons of life. The Lord said we will inherit His promises *"through faith and patience"* (Hebrews 6:12).

At the start of every new year, people make all kinds of resolutions—starting an exercise routine...getting out of debt...losing some weight...strengthening relationships. These are all well and good, but there's another resolution I encourage you to put at the very *top* of your list today:

**Resolve that in the coming months
you will develop a more intimate personal
relationship with the Lord!**

No matter what season of life you've been in recently, God wants you to develop a firm spiritual foundation so you can confidently stand when you are buffeted by the storms of life

(Matthew 7:24-29). Don't wait until you see the storm clouds start to gather before you decide you need a strong relationship with the Lord!

YOUR NEW BEGINNING IS COMING!

Although it may seem like it's a long way off, your springtime is just around the corner. God offers you a springtime of greater vision, deeper roots, and more powerful answers to prayer. The more difficult your winter season has been, the greater your coming harvest can be!

As you trust God and persevere through the winter season, a whole New Beginning can be yours...new joy...new peace...and new victory in Christ. Don't give up!

God is challenging you today: "Forget the past. Forget the failures. Forget the mistakes. Just come and walk closely with Me, and I will give you a New Beginning and help you walk in triumph and abundance." How can you resist a loving God like that?

Am I promising that life will always be easy after your New Beginning? Not at all. The storms of life will continue to blow from time to time...in your life...in your family...in your nation...and in the world.

However, you can resolve to build your life's foundation on the firm ground of Christ's love and faithfulness. Then when storms hit, you won't collapse but will stand firm in the knowledge, safety, and protection of your Lord and Savior.

My friend, don't wait until there's a crisis and then run to Jesus, pleading, "Save me from this situation!" Instead, call upon the Lord *NOW* for the New Beginning you need. Get to know Him better, and learn to hear the voice of His Holy Spirit. If you do this, you can be confident of victory no matter what adversity might come your way.

REMEMBER WHAT SPRINGTIME LOOKS LIKE

Perhaps you've been stuck in your winter season so long that you've practically forgotten what spring looks like. If so, let me share a precious reminder of the Lord's "springtime" love for you:

> *Rise up, my love, my fair one,*
> *And come away.*
> *For lo, **the winter is past,***
> *The rain is over and gone.*
> *The flowers appear on the earth;*
> *The **time of singing has come.***
> (Song of Solomon 2:10-12)

This is God's word to YOU today, my friend. He is calling you to *rise up*, because your winter season is giving way to a springtime of New Beginnings…new life…and joyous singing!

 ## *Searching Your Heart*

1. Describe a "winter season" in which you have found yourself stuck.

2. What are the Godly and ungodly responses you've had to these challenging circumstances?

3. With God's help, make a list of the areas of your life in which you need a New Beginning.

4. Spend time now talking with God about your winter season.

   - Worship and thank Him for how He has sustained you during your winter seasons.

   - Repent for any ungodly coping methods you've used that may have hurt Him, yourself, or others during these difficult seasons.

   - Offer your New Beginnings list to Him, asking Him to lead you into a New Beginning in each area, in His perfect timing and perfect way.

DON'T
WASTE *Your*
ADVERSITY

WHILE YOU AWAIT YOUR SPRINGTIME breakthrough—
your New Beginning—remember that God wants to use *every*
season of your life to bless you. Even the winter seasons are
intended for your good.

While spring and summer are times of *upward* growth, winter is a time of *downward* growth. In the winter, instead of trees
growing upward, their roots are growing deeper into the soil.

God uses the winter seasons to provide you with an opportunity to let your roots grow deeper in Christ. Too often, we pray
for a trouble-free Christian life, but deep roots usually develop
in the winter seasons, during the times of adversity and testing.

Instead of wasting your winter seasons, you must use difficult times to develop your spiritual root system and get ready
for the great harvest God is preparing for your future!

A STRANGE WAY TO GROW TREES

I love the story about a man who had an unconventional
way of taking care of his trees:

> *Had an old neighbor when I was growing up named
> Doctor Gibbs. He didn't look like any doctor I'd ever
> known. Every time I saw him, he was wearing denim
> overalls and a straw hat, the front brim of which was green*

sunglass plastic. He smiled a lot, a smile that matched his hat—old and crinkly and well-worn. He never yelled at us for playing in his yard. I remember him as someone who was a lot nicer than circumstances warranted.

When Doctor Gibbs wasn't saving lives, he was planting trees. His house sat on ten acres, and his life-goal was to make it a forest. The good doctor had some interesting theories concerning plant husbandry. He came from the "No pain, no gain" school of horticulture. He never watered his new trees, which flew in the face of conventional wisdom.

Once I asked why he said that watering plants spoiled them, and that if you water them, each successive tree generation will grow weaker and weaker. So you have to make things rough for them and weed out the weenie trees early on. He talked about how watering trees made for shallow roots, and how trees that weren't watered had to grow deep roots in search of moisture. I took him to mean that deep roots were to be treasured.

So he never watered his trees. He'd plant an oak and, instead of watering it every morning, he'd beat it with a rolled up newspaper. Smack! Slap! Pow! I asked him why he did that, and he said it was to get the tree's attention.

Doctor Gibbs went to glory a couple years after I left home. Every now and again, I walk by his house and look at the trees that I'd watched him plant some twenty-five years ago. They're granite strong now—big and robust. Those trees wake up in the morning and beat their chests and drink their coffee black.

I planted a couple trees a few years back. Carried water to them for a solid summer. Sprayed them. Prayed over them. The whole nine yards. Two years of coddling has *resulted in trees that expect to be waited on hand and foot. Whenever a cold wind blows in, they tremble and chatter their branches. Sissy trees.*

Funny thing about those trees of Doctor Gibbs. Adversity and deprivation seemed to benefit them in ways comfort and ease never could.

Every night before I go to bed, I go check on my two sons. I stand over them and watch their little bodies, the rising and falling of life within. I often pray for them. Mostly I pray that their lives will be easy. "Lord, spare them from hardship." But lately I've been thinking that it's time to change my prayer.

Has to do with the inevitability of cold winds that hit us at the core. I know my children are going to encounter hardship, and my praying they won't is naive. There's always a cold wind blowing somewhere.

So I'm changing my eventide prayer. Because life is tough, whether we want it to be or not. Instead, I'm going to pray that my sons' roots grow deep, so they can draw strength from the hidden sources of the eternal God.

Too many times we pray for ease, but that's a prayer seldom met. What we need to do is pray for roots that reach deep into the Eternal, so when the rains fall and the winds blow, we won't be swept asunder.[1]

Isn't this a great story? Deep spiritual roots are important. The Lord is growing us to be strong in faith, strong in grace, and strong in the knowledge that He is in control of the circumstances of our lives. There must be times when our roots grow deeper so we can move into new dimensions in our relationship with Christ.

[1] "Growing Roots," from Philip Gulley's book *Front Porch Tales* (Multnomah), used by permission.

WINTER'S LESSONS

In winter, things often look dead—but they're not. When the season changes and spring comes, suddenly everything that appeared dead begins to bloom and come to life again. And, amazingly, everything looks bigger, stronger, and healthier than it did before the winter.

When winter comes in your life and you can't seem to feel God's presence...or it seems like nobody cares about you and you feel all alone...or the future seems uncertain, remember winter's lessons: Your life isn't over! God hasn't forgotten you! He hasn't moved away! He's giving you the opportunity to grow deeper roots!

Jesus promises that He will never leave you nor forsake you (Hebrews 13:5)! Even in your winter seasons, He assures you, *"I am with you ALWAYS, even to the end of the age"* (Matthew 28:20).

God brings you through difficult circumstances for a reason. Your times of adversity are designed...

- **To test and refine you.** Job testifies about this: *"God knows the way I take; when He has tried me, I shall come forth as gold"* (Job 23:10). And Paul tells us:

   We do not lose heart...for momentary, light affliction is producing for us an eternal weight of glory far beyond all comparison (2 Corinthians 4:16-17).

Don't lose heart today! You will come out of your winter season shining like gold!

- **To mold your character into the image of Christ.** Peter writes that each of us will experience some degree of suffering as we follow Christ: *"You have been called for this purpose, since Christ also suffered for you, leaving you* an example for you to follow in His steps (1 Peter 2:21). And Paul reminds us that God's grand purpose for our lives is to make us *"conformed to the image of His Son"* (Romans 8:29).

God is aware of your difficult situations, and He wants to work them all together for your good as you seek His purposes (Romans 8:28).

- **To deepen your spiritual roots.** Having deeper roots will help you withstand the storms of life (Luke 6:47-48) and bear more fruit for God's Kingdom. Solomon writes in Proverbs 12 that *"the root of the righteous will **not be moved"*** (v. 3) and *"the root of the righteous **yields fruit"*** (v. 12).

Those with deep spiritual roots recognize their dependency on the Holy Spirit, and this is something almost always gained during times of testing. If you never had any difficulties, you would never have anything to overcome. And how would you realize your need for the Lord's help if you never had a problem? You'd be tempted to rely on your own strength and be self-sufficient.

- **To fill you with greater compassion in ministering to others.** Paul explains this:

The Father of mercies and God of all comfort...comforts us in all our affliction so that we will be able to comfort those who are in any affliction with the comfort with which we ourselves are comforted by God (2 Corinthians 1:3-4).

Sometimes God allows tough circumstances in your life to demonstrate to you and those around you His majesty, power, glory, holiness, and faithfulness. The lessons you learn during the winter seasons of your life can be a powerful tool to minister to others during their difficult seasons.

GOD'S 'TOUGH LOVE'

Often we don't recognize that God allows adversity in our lives because He *loves* us. It's for our good, as this story from Zig Ziglar points out:

> *The giraffe is the largest mammal that gives birth while standing up. I don't speak "giraffe," but I can imagine what the baby giraffe must think when he bounces on the ground from that great height. He just left warm, cushioned quarters in which all his needs, comforts and security were provided. Now he finds himself bouncing off (comparatively speaking) hard, cold, unwelcoming ground.*
>
> *Almost immediately thereafter, a new trauma occurs in the baby giraffe's life. As he struggles to his knees, Mama Giraffe gets busy "persuading" him to stand up. She does this as he wobbles to his feet by giving him a swift kick to prod him to faster action.*
>
> *No sooner does he reach his feet than Mama delivers a booming kick that knocks the baby giraffe back down. I can well imagine the baby giraffe thinking, "Well, make up your mind, Mom! First you kicked me to make me stand up. Then you kicked me back down!"*
>
> *That process is repeated several times, because Mama Giraffe loves her baby. Mama Giraffe knows that the only chance for survival her baby has is to be able to quickly get up and move out of harm's way. Yes, kicking the baby up and down seems like a strange way to show love. But for a baby giraffe it is the ultimate expression of love.*

Caution: This approach definitely won't work in the "people" world, but the principle will. Real love is evidenced when you do what is best for the other person, whether or not they appreciate it at that moment.

God means your adversities and winter experiences for your good! They are meant to help you mature and become like Christ.

WHEN YOUR HOPE MUST WAIT

Proverbs 13:12 tells us, *"Hope deferred makes the heart sick, but desire fulfilled is a tree of life."* Sometimes it's easy to get a sick heart, especially when you've been hoping, praying, believing, and doing everything you think you're supposed to be doing—and you still don't see the answers to your prayers.

Maybe you've been hoping for God to send you a spouse...restore a broken relationship...reach a wayward son or daughter...heal a sick loved one...deliver you from an addiction...or give you a financial breakthrough. Perhaps you've grown weary and heartsick, because you still haven't seen the fulfillment of your hopes and prayers.

Don't give up, my friend. Keep believing. God is faithful, and your harvest is coming!

I've heard there's a certain type of Chinese bamboo plant that is planted as a sprout. Although you faithfully water and care for it, this plant shows no growth at all during the first year. Even in the second, third, and fourth years, there are no signs of growth. Despite your best efforts to care for the plant, it still doesn't look like anything is happening.

When you're just about ready to give up on this good-for-nothing plant, something amazing happens. In the fifth year, the plant grows 90 feet in just about five weeks!

Perhaps you've been waiting...a year...two years...three years...four years...but still no harvest. Don't lose heart! Your breakthrough may be just ahead!

If you have a sick heart today because your hopes haven't been realized, the Bible reminds you, *"Let us not grow weary while doing good, for in due season we shall reap if we do not lose heart"* (Galatians 6:9).

Don't become weary or heartsick as you await your harvest. God is faithful, and your New Beginning is at hand!

 *Searching Your Heart*

1. What have you been praying, waiting, and hoping for God to do in your life?

2. Has deferred hope made your heart sick (Proverbs 13:12)? If so, describe your "heart sickness" and the healing you're asking God to give you.

3. How has God used your winter season to cause your roots to grow deep in Him?

4. Spend time now talking with God about the breakthroughs you're waiting for Him to provide.

   - Thank Him for using your winter seasons to cause your roots in Him to grow deeper and stronger.

   - Ask Him to heal your "heart sickness" and renew your hope in Him.

   - Memorize Galatians 6:9: *"Let us not grow weary while doing good, for in due season we shall reap if we do not lose heart,"* asking Him to encourage and strengthen your heart with this verse.

*You're on
your way to
a wonderful
new life.*

WHERE ARE *You?*

WHEN GOD CREATED THE EARTH, He didn't seek advice from the angels, call a committee meeting, or take a vote. He simply spoke...and His words were so full of life, so powerful, so undeniable that everything came into being immediately.

There was never a question as to God's authority or His ability to create the heavens and the earth, but the first question in the Bible came as Satan planted seeds of doubt concerning the integrity of God's Word:

> *Now the serpent was more crafty than any beast of the field which the LORD God had made. And he said to the woman, "Indeed, **has God said,** 'You shall not eat from any tree of the garden'?"*

Satan's initial question didn't directly call God a liar, but that was soon to follow:

> *And the woman said to the serpent, "From the fruit of the trees of the garden we may eat; but from the fruit of the tree which is in the middle of the garden, God has said, 'You shall not eat from it or touch it, lest you die.'"*

> *And the serpent said to the woman, "**You surely shall not die!** For God knows that in the day you eat from it your eyes will be opened, and you will be like God, knowing good and evil* (Genesis 3:1-3).

Note that the devil didn't seem to make a *major* revision in God's warning about the forbidden fruit—he just rearranged the word *"not"*! God had said, "You shall *'not'* eat...or you shall surely die." The devil said, "You shall eat...and you surely shall *'not'* die."

How could such a small revision make such a big difference? One version was truth—the other was a lie! The nearest cemetery is a silent witness as to who was telling the truth. The disobedience of Adam and Eve brought spiritual and physical death to the human race—just as God had warned.

THE SECOND QUESTION

The second question in the Bible is one that has been repeated again and again throughout the centuries... *"Where are you?"* This is the question God asked Adam in Genesis 3:9 when Adam was hiding in the bushes—and the Lord continues to ask us this same question today.

Make no mistake about it: God knows exactly where we are! He wasn't looking for missing persons when He asked Adam and Eve, *"Where are you?"* He knew where they were hiding, but He wanted them to understand the full ramifications of what they had done. God wanted them to experience the painful realization that they were now alienated from Him. He wanted them to see that they were accountable for their actions.

Just as He asked Adam and Eve, the Lord is asking you today: *"Where are you?"* How are you going to answer Him? Are you walking right beside Him, or are you hiding somewhere behind the "bushes" of denial and blame-shifting?

When the Lord asks that question, many people choose the route Adam tried: blame-shifting. Adam replied, *"The woman whom You gave to be with me, she gave me from the tree, and I ate"* (Genesis 3:12).

Instead of taking any responsibility himself, Adam blamed God because He brought Eve into his life, and he blamed Eve for giving him the forbidden fruit. Meanwhile, Eve blamed the serpent (Genesis 3:13).

But God didn't buy any of their excuses. He wanted Adam and Eve to see that their predicament was brought about as a result of *choices* they had made.

If you don't like the place where you find yourself today, don't blame your spouse...children...church...pastor...job... boss...age...race... education...or even the devil! The starting place for your New Beginning is to accept responsibility for the decisions that have brought you to this place you're in.

LOCATION OR DESTINATION?

I like what a pastor in Colorado tells his congregation: "Think of where you are as your *location,* not your *destination!"* Just as David said he would *"walk through the valley of the shadow of death"* (Psalm 23:4), you need to *"walk through"* your present location...

- If you're going through a *winter season* in your life, you can pass through to *springtime.*

- If you have a *strained relationship* in your marriage or with your children, God can help you pass through to a New Beginning of *healthy relationships.*

- If you're experiencing *financial struggles,* God wants you to break through to His *prosperity.*

- If you're walking through a time of *illness* in your body, God wants to touch you with His *healing* power.

- If you find yourself *depressed* or *lonely*, God can give you His *peace* and *joy*.

Whatever difficult situation you may be "passing through" today, remember that it's only your location—not your destination. Don't quit walking! Keep on trusting the Lord! Don't stop until you've laid hold of your New Beginning.

You've probably known many people who "camp out" in their valleys instead of passing through to their New Beginning. Instead of trusting and praising the Lord, they wallow in their circumstances and hold a pity party.

We all have painful experiences along the roads of life—and we all have choices to make about how we will respond. We can moan and groan and blame everyone we've ever met, but the fact remains: We probably have come to our present location largely because of the choices we've made.

So why not make a choice to have a New Beginning?

ENOUGH IS ENOUGH

Are you ready to leave your present location and embrace your New Beginning? Are you ready to say to yourself, "I've had enough! No more excuses...no more passing the buck...no more playing the blame game. I'm sick and tired of saying, hearing, doing, and getting the same old things out of life"?

Remember this: You'll never change what you are unwilling to confront.

When you come to this point of facing the truth about your situation and of being willing to do whatever it takes to move on, your New Beginning is right around the corner! You can experience the reality of this powerful truth from the apostle Paul:

If anyone is in Christ, he is a new creature: old things are passed away; behold, all things have become new (2 Corinthians 5:17).

Being *"in Christ"* means more than making a New Year's resolution, turning over a new leaf, or adopting a more positive mental attitude. Being *"in Christ"* means surrendering to Jesus as the Lord of your life and following His directives. It means a willingness to leave the past behind so God can give you His New Beginning.

DON'T STAY WHERE YOU ARE!

If where you are today is not where you want to be, remember that it's only your location, not your destination! You don't have to stay where you are!

Are you stuck in the quagmire of yesterday's faults, failures, and sins? Are you held captive by the opinions of narrow-minded, small-thinking people? Have you allowed your life to be tossed to and fro by the howling winds of adversity?

If you've taken up residence in the valley of unfulfilled promises and broken dreams, it's time to move on! Instead of allowing the devil to taunt you with thoughts about what might have been, listen to God's prophetic voice about your glorious future!

New Beginnings are not for fault-finders, excuse-makers, wanna-bees or gonna-bees! New Beginnings are reserved for men and women who will dare to be different in a world of cookie-cutter copies—those who dare to dream big while multitudes around them wallow in unbelief and mediocrity.

New Beginnings are for those brave hearts who look for silver linings in every cloud and rainbows after every storm.

They stake their hopes in tomorrow rather than yesterday, and they expect to be known by their future instead of their past.

New Beginnings are for those who have fizzled, flopped, and failed, but have chosen to rise from the ashes of defeat to soar on eagles' wings. It's for those who have loved and lost and lived to love again.

New Beginnings are for people like YOU—who are willing to leave the past behind in order to press toward God's high calling for you in Christ. But you need to get started on the right foot...

 *Searching Your Heart*

1. Describe your present relationship with the Lord. Are you walking with Him or hiding from Him? What needs to change?

2. Ask the Lord to show you any ways you've been refusing to take responsibility or blaming others for your current circumstances. Be honest with yourself and with Him. Write down what He reveals to you and repent for each one.

3. Think about your responses to these questions: Are you truly ready to choose to make a New Beginning in God? Are you willing now to surrender everything to Jesus and make Him the Lord of your life? Will you obey Him and follow His direction?

4. Spend time now talking with God about the choices you've been making.

   - Worship Him for His goodness and mercy toward you, even in the midst of any wrong choices you have made.

   - Ask Him for the wisdom and courage to make right choices that will result in your New Beginning.

   - Praise Him in advance for the glorious future He has in store for you!

God's Word
gives us strength
for the day.

START *Your* NEW BEGINNING GOD'S WAY

AT THE TURN OF EVERY NEW YEAR, millions of people enthusiastically proclaim their joy that another year is over and they can begin again with a clean slate. Celebrating with their friends, they party the night away and inevitably make resolutions they have no real intention of keeping.

Is this really a New Beginning? No, instead of being a New Beginning, it's simply an old form of insanity: doing the same thing over and over, but expecting different results!

Most New Year's resolutions are just *counterfeit* New Beginnings. Lots of talk...but little action. Usually there's a temporary effort to change...but no long-term follow-through or commitment. Gyms and fitness centers are typically packed for a week or two into the new year, but then reality sets in and the crowds are gone.

Half-hearted resolutions clearly won't work. If you want a New Beginning that is genuine and lasting, you need to honestly assess your life and make a firm commitment to the Lordship of Jesus Christ. You must recognize and reject the devil's seductive siren song—his scheme to steal, kill, and destroy the Lord's purposes and blessings in your life (John 10:10).

IT STARTS WITH REPENTANCE

A lasting transformation always begins with *repentance.*

Repentance simply means "to change your mind...the way you think." Repentance involves a firm decision to allow God to rule over your thoughts, attitudes, and actions. It means turning from Satan's lies and embracing God's truth.

The key to repentance is not necessarily an emotional, tear-filled response, but simply a DECISION...an act of your will. God isn't moved by your tears unless He has full access to your *heart.*

The test of repentance, ultimately, is FRUIT. John the Baptist wasn't overly impressed when some of the religious leaders came to him for baptism. Rather, he challenged them to *"bear fruit in keeping with repentance"* (Matthew 3:8). When you've truly repented, your life will change and you'll begin to go in the opposite direction from your sinful past.

We see a similar scene in Acts 2, when the Holy Spirit was poured out and Peter preached to the crowd gathered for the Day of Pentecost. Many in the crowd were deeply moved by Peter's message, and they cried out, *"What shall we do?"* (v. 37)

Perhaps that's the question you're asking as you read this book. You yearn for a New Beginning and sense God working in your heart, but you wonder, "What shall I do to get started?"

Look at Peter's answer to the crowd:

> *"**Repent,** and each of you be baptized in the name of Jesus Christ for the forgiveness of your sins; and you will receive the gift of the Holy Spirit. For the promise is for you and your children and for all who are far off, as many as the Lord our God will call to Himself."*
>
> *And with many other words he solemnly testified and kept on exhorting them, saying, "Be saved from this perverse generation!"* (Acts 2:38-40)

If you want a New Beginning and a lifestyle that reflects

being *"saved from this perverse generation,"* your first step is to repent and receive God's forgiveness and the empowerment of His Spirit.

RECEIVE GOD'S FORGIVENESS

Note that forgiveness is a gift, not something you can merit or earn. If you have sinned and failed God in some way, simply ask Him to forgive you. He sent His Son to die for your sins. By the shed blood of Jesus, the total price for your salvation was paid, and all God requires of you is to believe in His Son and receive everlasting, never-ending life!

If you have never turned from your sins and self-centered ways to surrender your life to Jesus Christ, I encourage you to take a few minutes right now to make sure He is your Lord and Savior. You don't need to say a flowery or complicated prayer, but simply open your heart's door wide to Christ. The Holy Spirit will lead you in what to say, but here's a simple prayer for you to consider:

> *Lord Jesus, thank You for dying for my sins so I can be forgiven and can have a personal relationship with You. I believe You are the Son of God and that God raised You from the dead. I turn from my own ways and ask You to come into my heart and be the Lord of my life. I surrender my thoughts and actions to You. Please give me the New Beginning and abundant life You promise.*

If you prayed this prayer with a sincere heart, you are well on your way to a New Beginning!

A RENEWED MIND

Many new Christians misunderstand the new birth (John

3:1-8) and Paul's statement that those in Christ become *"new creations"* (2 Corinthians 5:17). They expect every area of their lives to change instantly at their conversion.

While God often brings about dramatic and immediate changes when you are saved, He also wants you to realize that some transformations are a *process*. For example, in Romans 12:2, Paul says you are *"transformed by the renewing of your mind."* As a result, *"we have the mind of Christ"* (1 Corinthians 2:16).

This process begins when you first repent, but Paul is addressing his statement to many Believers who have already walked with the Lord for quite a while. The message is clear: Your mind will steadily be renewed as you make a daily commitment to study and obey God's Word, and as you allow His Holy Spirit to shape your thoughts and actions.

Think of it this way: When a baby is born, he doesn't come into the world walking and talking. His memory is a blank slate. He has to *learn* to walk and *learn* to talk.

Over time the baby develops mentally, physically, and emotionally. Maturity takes place. New skills are learned.

It's the same with the New Birth (John 3:1-7). When a person surrenders their life to Christ and asks Him to be the Lord of their life, old things are supposed to pass away and all things are supposed to become new.

BE PATIENT WITH THE GROWTH PROCESS

Some people experience an immediate transformation in the passing away of old things. For example, many people who have been addicted to drugs or alcohol find they're immediately set free from their bondage to these chains. For others, finding freedom from these old things takes time.

Many people sincerely want a New Beginning with God, yet they become discouraged when the changes don't happen all at once. They haven't taken time to let their mind be renewed, nor have they understood the many verses challenging Christians to see spiritual growth as a process that requires perseverance, growth, and self-discipline:

> *Like newborn babies, long for the pure milk of the word, so that by it you may **grow** in respect to salvation* (1 Peter 2:2).

> ***Grow** in the grace and knowledge of our Lord and Savior Jesus Christ* (2 Peter 3:18).

> ***Discipline** yourself for the purpose of godliness* (1 Timothy 4:7).

> *Let us run with **endurance** the race that is set before us, fixing our eyes on Jesus, the author and perfecter of our faith* (Hebrews 12:1-2).

> *Be imitators of those who through **faith** and **patience** inherit the promises* (Hebrews 6:12).

Many other verses could be cited to show that spiritual growth and transformation is a process rather than a one-time event.

I love this promise from Proverbs 4:18: "*The path of the righteous is like the light of dawn, that shines brighter and brighter until the full day.*" Once your New Beginning starts, God wants the light of your testimony to grow brighter and brighter until all can see the incredible transformation He has brought about in your life!

EVERYTHING YOU NEED

Spiritual growth requires perseverance and self-discipline, but it isn't some kind of self-help program. Instead of "pulling yourself up by your bootstraps," God wants you to tap into His supernatural strength.

Paul tells the Ephesian Christians that they will certainly face spiritual battles along the way, but he encourages them to *"be strong in the Lord and in the strength of His might"* (Ephesians 6:10). Likewise, God challenges Joshua, *"Be strong and courageous! Do not tremble or be dismayed, for the LORD your God is with you wherever you go"* (Joshua 1:9).

Your New Beginning doesn't depend on YOU being strong...it depends on tapping into GOD'S STRENGTH! Peter, likewise, encourages you that God makes His supernatural power available and offers everything you need to experience an abundant Christian life:

> **His divine power** has granted to us **everything** pertaining to life and godliness, through the true knowledge of Him who called us by His own glory and excellence (2 Peter 1:3).

What a great promise! You can know today that God offers you EVERYTHING you need for your New Beginning!

LAY HOLD OF GOD'S POWER

Remember, New Beginnings aren't automatic. Although, God's *"divine power"* is available to you today, you still must lay hold of it by faith and obedience. If you continue to do what you've always done, you'll continue to get what you've always gotten. Purpose in your heart that *nothing* will stop you from receiving the full measure of God's blessings.

Do you feel the change in the air? Your winter season may seem in full strength, but springtime is just around the corner. Make today the start of your New Beginning as you fully surrender your life to the Lord.

 *Searching Your Heart*

1. Make a list of past resolutions you've made but failed to keep. What caused you to fail to meet these goals?

2. What is the relationship between repentance and making a New Beginning?

3. Paul says in Romans 12:2 that we need to be transformed by the renewing of our minds. How does *your* mind need to be transformed and renewed?

4. Spend time now talking with God about repentance and renewing your mind.

   - Express your gratitude to Him for the gift of His Son Jesus Christ, Who has made it possible for your sins to be forgiven and for your mind to be transformed.

   - Ask God to reveal to you the sins you need to repent of in order to experience a New Beginning. Ask Him to forgive you in Jesus' name for each one.

   - Choose one of the verses from this chapter to memorize. Call it to mind in the days ahead as a way to renew your mind and gain the mind of Christ.

BE EMPOWERED FOR *Your* NEW BEGINNING

AS SOON AS YOU'VE REPENTED OF YOUR OLD WAYS and asked God to give you a New Beginning, you're on your way to a wonderful new life. However, there still are some crucial steps that you need to take.

Let's take another look at Peter's concluding message to the crowd gathered at Pentecost:

> *"Repent, and each of you **be baptized** in the name of Jesus Christ for the forgiveness of your sins; and you will **receive the gift of the Holy Spirit"** (Acts 2:38).*

Repentance was the first step Peter mentioned for a New Beginning, but he also challenged the crowd to demonstrate their repentance by water baptism and the empowerment of the Holy Spirit.

BURY YOUR OLD LIFE

Water baptism is a wonderful picture of a New Beginning. It illustrates the burial of our old life of sin and then our resurrection to a new life in Christ. Paul explains:

> *We have been buried with Him through baptism into death, so that as Christ was raised from the dead*

*through the glory of the Father, so we too might walk
in newness of life.*

*For if we have become united with Him in the likeness
of His death, certainly we shall also be in the likeness
of His resurrection, knowing this, that our old self
was crucified with Him, in order that our body of sin
might be done away with, so that we would no longer be
slaves to sin…Even so consider yourselves to be dead to
sin, but alive to God in Christ Jesus* (Romans 6:4-11).

Notice that Paul doesn't say a New Beginning is a matter of just "trying harder." It means dying to your old life and considering yourself buried with Christ. Instead of merely "turning over a new leaf," God wants you to *"walk in newness of life."*

If you've never been baptized in water as a Believer—testifying to the world, the flesh, and the devil that you are burying your old life and rising to a new life in Christ—I encourage you to take this vital step. When done in faith and with an understanding of its full meaning, water baptism is a powerful way to cut off the shackles of your old life and any remaining Satanic strongholds.

YOU NEED THE POWER

Peter also told the crowd that they should start their New Beginning by receiving *"the gift of the Holy Spirit"* (Acts 2:38). You can be certain that the enemy will try to rob you of your New Beginning, but God wants to empower you to live in victory and abundance. He wants to give you the power of His Spirit, not as a luxury but as a necessity!

Before His ascension, Jesus told the disciples they must be empowered to be His witnesses: *"You will receive **power** when* *the Holy Spirit has come upon you; and you shall be **My** witnesses both in Jerusalem, and in all Judea and Samaria, and even to the remotest part of the earth"* (Acts 1:8).

You don't need to settle for a powerless and defeated Christian life! Jesus said, *"You **WILL** receive power"!* Receiving the power of the Holy Spirit is essential to walking victoriously in your New Beginning day by day.

Receiving the power of the Holy Spirit isn't some kind of strange or spooky spiritual experience. It's a NORMAL and NECESSARY part of the Christian life.

Paul told the Ephesians, *"Do not get drunk with wine, for that is dissipation, but be filled with the Spirit"* (Ephesians 5:18). If you are struggling with addiction to alcohol, drugs, food, gambling, pornography, or any other kind of bondage today, this is your key to being an overcomer: *"Be filled with the Spirit"!* Instead of being controlled by some kind of addiction, let your life be controlled by the Holy Spirit of God.

THE CHOICE IS YOURS

Victory in the Christian life isn't automatic. God offers us His supernatural power, but we also have choices to make in order to appropriate that power.

Paul tells us, *"The mind set on the flesh is death, but the mind set on the Spirit is life and peace"* (Romans 8:6). That means we must *choose* where we *"set"* our mind. Even as Believers, we have a daily decision to make about whether we'll listen to the voice of God or the voice of the enemy.

The *"deeds of the flesh"* are ugly and displeasing to God: *"immorality, impurity, sensuality, idolatry, sorcery, enmities, strife, jealousy, outbursts of anger, disputes, dissensions, factions, envying, drunkenness, carousing, and things like these"*

(Galatians 5:19-21). If these are the qualities that characterize your life today, I have one word for you: STOP! If you're a child of God, you don't need to live that way.

In contrast, the Lord offers to fill your life with *"the fruit of the Spirit"*: *"love, joy, peace, patience, kindness, goodness, faithfulness, gentleness, self-control"* (Galatians 5:22-23).

Which will you choose? The deeds of the flesh or the fruit of the Spirit? It's all a matter of where you set your mind and heart.

THE ANOINTING BRINGS FREEDOM

The Holy Spirit not only gives us *"power from on high"* (Luke 24:49), but He also delivers us from demonic bondage. Shortly after He was empowered by the Spirit at His baptism by John in the Jordan River, Jesus entered a synagogue and read this Scripture passage from Isaiah:

> *The Spirit of the LORD is upon Me,*
> *Because He anointed Me to preach the gospel to the poor.*
> *He has sent Me to proclaim **release to the captives**,*
> *And recovery of sight to the blind,*
> *To **set free those who are oppressed**,*
> *To proclaim the favorable year of the LORD* (Luke 4:18).

If you've been a captive to sin or Satan in some area of your life, please hear this: By the power of the Holy Spirit, Jesus offers release to captives! Because of the anointing of the Spirit, Jesus will *"set free those who are oppressed."*

The freedom Jesus offers is not temporary or transitory. The Bible declares, *"If the Son sets you free, you will be free indeed"* (John 8:36)!

You don't need to live your life in bondage to sin or Satan. Remember these great promises from God's Word:

The Son of God appeared for this purpose, to destroy the works of the devil (1 John 3:8).

Greater is He [Jesus] who is in you than he who is in the world [Satan] (1 John 4:4).

I have been crucified with Christ; and it is no longer I who live, but Christ lives in me (Galatians 2:20).

I can do all things through Him who strengthens me (Philippians 4:13).

God offers you the power to be an overcomer! Be filled with the Holy Spirit!

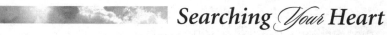 ## *Searching Your Heart*

1. Have you ever been baptized in water as a Believer? Write down your memory of this special event in your life.

2. If you haven't been water baptized, write down the steps you're going to take this week so you can be baptized as a symbol of the New Beginning you're making in Jesus Christ.

3. Have you been filled with the power of God's Holy Spirit? Write down when this happened and the difference it has made in your daily walk with the Lord.

4. If you've never asked God to fill you with the power of His Holy Spirit, you can do so now just by praying this prayer:

   God, thank You for sending Jesus to save me from my sins. Jesus, I want You to be Lord over every area of my life. Thank You for sending Your Holy Spirit so I can be empowered to walk victoriously in a New Beginning with You day by day.

   Holy Spirit, in Jesus' name, I invite You to come and fill me up right now. Thank You for Your spiritual gifts and the fruits of love, joy, peace, patience, kindness, goodness, faithfulness, gentleness, and self-control.

   Father God, thank You for Your Holy Spirit. Jesus, I pray this prayer in Your powerful name. Amen.

5. Sit quietly now in God's presence, worshipping Him and thanking Him for filling you with His Holy Spirit. Ask Him to give you the words to praise Him in Jesus' name.

GET OUT
OF JAIL—FREE

If you've ever played the popular board game, *Monopoly*, you've probably received a "Get Out of Jail Free" card. Instead of trying to pay your way out of jail, that single card was your ticket to instant freedom.

Although many Believers don't realize it, God has given each of us a "Get Out of Jail Free" card. Jesus' death on the Cross makes it possible for us to escape from our prison of sin and death! People may try all sorts of other things to help them overcome their winter season and find a New Beginning, but only Jesus' blood can truly cleanse our sins and set us free.

I love the old hymn by Robert Lowry:

What can wash away my sin?
Nothing but the blood of Jesus.
What can make me whole again?
Nothing but the blood of Jesus.

O precious is the flow
That makes me white as snow;
No other fount I know;
Nothing but the blood of Jesus.

If God has forgiven your shortcomings and sins, why should

YOU remember them? If the devil keeps sowing condemnation in your life by bringing up your painful or sinful past, remember this: The devil is a liar! God's Word says, *"There is therefore now NO condemnation for those who are in Christ Jesus"* (Romans 8:1)!

On the Cross, Jesus bore all your fears, guilt, and shame…so YOU don't have to bear them any longer! Once you grasp this truth, you will not only be free from the "jailhouse" of your past, but also free to go forward in God and experience a New Beginning in Him.

What a blessing to receive God's "Get Out of Jail Free" card! So toss that guilt, fear, shame, or condemnation out of your life, out of your mind, and out of your spirit, and come into God's presence with praise and worship on your lips!

DON'T GO BACK TO JAIL

It breaks God's heart that many of His children have "gone back to jail." He has graciously forgiven their sins, but they've allowed unforgiveness toward others to bring them back into a spiritual prison.

In Matthew 18:21-35 Jesus tells a sobering story about a man who was forgiven from a huge debt, but who refused to forgive someone who owed him a much smaller amount. The man had come before his master to plead for mercy, and the master was gracious to him: *"The master of that servant was moved with compassion, released him, and forgave him the debt"* (v. 27).

Friend, this is exactly what the Lord has done for YOU in Jesus' death on the Cross…

- He showed His compassion for you.

- He forgave your debt of sin.

- He released you from the prison of your past.

Unfortunately, though, this story doesn't have a happy ending. This man who received such mercy refused to forgive someone who owed him a very small debt:

> *That servant went out and found one of his fellow servants who owed him a hundred denarii; and he laid hands on him and took him by the throat, saying, "Pay me what you owe!" So his fellow servant fell down at his feet and begged him, saying, "Have patience with me, and I will pay you all." And he would not, but went and threw him into prison till he should pay the debt* (vs. 28-30).

Notice that forgiving others is a *choice*, not a feeling. When asked for mercy, he was *unwilling* to give it. Although he had been set free from his own debt, he chose to put the other man in prison.

However, the master of the first servant was irate when he heard about this:

> *Then his master, after he had called him, said to him, "You wicked servant! I forgave you all that debt because you begged me. Should you not also have had compassion on your fellow servant, just as I had pity on you?"* (vs. 32-33)

The master's anger resulted in terrible consequences for the man who refused to forgive: "*His master was angry, and delivered him to the* **torturers** *until he should pay all that was due to him*" (v. 34).

Jesus ends this story with a pointed warning about the consequences of unforgiveness: "*My heavenly Father will also do the same to you, if each of you does not forgive his brother from your heart"* (v. 35).

ARE YOU BEING TORMENTED?

Jesus' story says those who hold on to unforgiveness will be handed over to *"torturers."* Other translations say *"tormenters"* or *"jailers."*

This isn't God's will for our lives! Jesus died to set us free from jail…free from guilt, shame, and torment. But our unwillingness to forgive others will bring us back into a jailhouse of our own making. The "Get Out of Jail Free" card will only work when we have forgiven everyone who has wronged us.

Jesus' story is an illustration of a warning He gives in the Sermon on the Mount. After instructing us to pray, *"Forgive us our debts, as we also have forgiven our debtors"* (Matthew 6:12), Jesus says, *"For if you forgive others for their transgressions, your heavenly Father will also forgive you. But if you do not forgive others, then your Father will not forgive your transgressions"* (vs. 14-15).

So many people today are being tormented by their past… their failures and mistakes…or the ways they've been victimized by another person. Sometimes the past traumas are very real, very severe, and very painful. Perhaps you've been victimized by an abusive relationship or a dishonest business partner. If so, God wants to wrap His love and compassion around you today—but He still requires you to forgive the person who wronged you.

If you find yourself in a place of torment today, God wants to release you. But the key to your prison is in your *own* hand. I encourage you today to get away for some time with the Lord, asking Him to work His forgiveness in your heart. As long as it

takes, spend time choosing to forgive each person who has hurt
you. Tear up every "IOU," and release them from their debts.

OFFENSES AND OBJECTIONS

Perhaps you've been holding on to your offenses for a long
time. Someone has hurt you deeply, and you feel justified in
holding an angry grudge against them. If so, there are two
things I want you to remember:

1. The main person hurt by your offense is not the other
   person, it's YOU!

2. As severely as you have been wronged, your trauma is
   no greater than was experienced by many men and
   women of God in the Bible:

   - Because of the jealousy of his brothers, **Joseph** was
     thrown into the bottom of a well, became a slave in
     Egypt, and spent years in a dungeon. Yet he chose to
     forgive his brothers and welcome them into the
     prosperity God had given him. Instead of taking
     revenge against his brothers, Joseph told them, *"You
     meant evil against me, but God meant it for good"*
     (Genesis 50:20).

   - **Job** found a wonderful reversal of his fortunes when
     he prayed for his friends—even though they had
     spent many days badgering and criticizing him (Job
     42:10-12).

   - **Naomi** and **Ruth** faced grief and uncertainty after
     their husbands died, yet God gave them a wonderful
     New Beginning when they moved back to Judah
     (Ruth 1:1-22).

- The **Samaritan woman at the well** (John 4:1-42) and the **woman caught in adultery** (John 8:1-11) both endured trauma at the hands of men and because of their own foolish choices—but they each received a New Beginning when Jesus forgave and restored them.

- The **widow at Zarephath** faced severe financial lack and the possibility of starvation, but she found God's supernatural provision when she sacrificially provided for Elijah (1 Kings 17:8-16).

- **Stephen** forgave those who were stoning him to death: *"Lord, do not hold this sin against them!"* (Acts 7:54-60) This act of forgiveness was one of the primary factors leading to the conversion of the apostle Paul.

- **Jesus**, while carrying the sins of the world on His back on the Cross, issued a powerful word of forgiveness that has echoed down through the centuries: *"Father, forgive them; for they do not know what they are doing"* (Luke 23:34).

So remember this when you're tempted to throw yourself a pity party and hold on to offenses toward others: God wants you to follow Jesus' example and forgive those who have treated you unjustly.

HURTFUL WAYS

Forgiveness often is very difficult, but it's an essential key to your New Beginning. Your winter season will go on *forever* unless you make a decision to forgive everyone who has hurt you.

David prayed, *"Search me, O God, and know my heart; try me and know my anxious thoughts; and see if there be any hurtful way in me"* (Psalm 139:23-24). Make no mistake about it, unforgiveness is a *"hurtful way"* that will imprison you with torment unless you deal with it.

Barbara and I recently spent time with a pastor friend of ours. He mentioned that each month he goes away for a few days to spend time with the Lord.

Barbara and I asked him what he did on these personal retreats, and he told us he always starts by asking the Lord to show him anyone he hadn't forgiven yet. Our friend shared that on one of these retreats, he spent *three whole days* forgiving people who had wronged him!

Like this pastor, don't just *assume* you've forgiven people who have hurt you. You may need to spend some time asking God to search your heart. If you're still *talking about* the offense—months or even years after it occurred—it's likely that you still have some forgiving to do.

Take time today to allow the Lord to search your heart and remove any *"hurtful way"* or unforgiveness that is keeping you imprisoned to your past.

LET GO!

I once heard a story about a mom who baked some chocolate chip cookies for her young son. "Tommy," she told him, "I'm putting the cookies in the cookie jar, but you can have some after dinner."

Of course, Tommy couldn't wait for this special treat. While his mom was in the other room, Tommy opened the cookie jar and reached in to grab a few big cookies. However, when he tried to remove his hand, he discovered that it was stuck.

Tommy began to cry and then screamed to his mom, "HELP! I'M TRAPPED!"

When Tommy's mom ran into the room, she saw that his hand was stuck, and he was sobbing hysterically. She decided the only option was to break open the cookie jar so he could get his hand out.

When she broke the jar, Tommy's mom was shocked to discover he was still clutching three cookies in his little hand. "Tommy, why didn't you *let go* of the cookies?!" she asked in amazement.

"But I *wanted* them!" Tommy replied as he broke into tears again.

If you find yourself stuck in a winter season today, you may need to let go of some "cookies" you've held on to. God wants to set you free from anything that has bound you and hindered your New Beginning, but you need to *let go*.

Like Tommy, you may be tempted to protest that the cookies you're grasping are something desirable and *good*—not something negative. But remember that *anything* is negative if it keeps us from God's *best* for our life. Paul says, *"Whatever things were gain to me, those things I have **counted as loss** for the sake of Christ"* (Philippians 3:7).

Today God offers you His "Get Out of Jail—Free" card, but you must let go of anything holding you back from your spiritual freedom in Jesus Christ. Once your surrender is complete, you'll be amazed by how quickly your New Beginning comes into view.

 *Searching Your Heart*

1. Consider your past and current circumstances. Are you living in freedom today, or are you living as though you're in a spiritual jail? Write down any insights God gives you about this.

2. In Matthew 18:21-35, Jesus tells a story that compares unforgiveness to being tormented and tortured. What memories of past or current hurts, wounds, and betrayals are tormenting and torturing you today?

3. Make a list of those who have hurt you, and ask God to show you whether you need to forgive them for the first time or forgive them again.

4. Spend time now talking with God about being set free from all these offenses.

   ▪ Thank God that since He has forgiven you, you are now able to forgive those who have caused you pain.

   ▪ Go through the list you made of those who have hurt you, and one-by-one forgive each person for what they did to cause you pain. As you do, repent for any anger, bitterness, or desire for revenge that may still be in your heart.

   ▪ Today and in the days ahead, when the enemy tries to remind you of these past hurts, remind *him* that you have chosen to forgive these people as God has forgiven you, and that you are now free in Jesus' name!

He wants to show you His purpose and provision.

FORGET
THE PAST

YOU PROBABLY HAVE MET PEOPLE WHO LOVE to live in the past. Day after day, they nurse old wounds and relive past tragedies. They recall in great detail every time they were maligned and mistreated.

Often these people struggle to find intimacy, for they're haunted by memories of trusted people who abused them. It's hard for them to trust God, because they recall a prayer 20 years ago that He didn't seem to answer. And they find it hard to participate in a church, because they can't get over the hypocrisies of other Christians.

What do you say to people who are so bound by the heartaches of their yesterdays that they miss the great plans God has for their life today? How can they shake off the shackles of the past and experience God's New Beginning?

ESCAPING THE PIG PEN

The life of the Prodigal Son reached a turning point when he *"came to himself"* while feeding pigs (Luke 15:17). He realized he was reaping the bitter fruit of his poor choices. If he stayed on his current path, his life would surely continue its downhill slide.

Until a person comes to this kind of moment of realization, he will continue to wallow in the pigpen of yesterday's faults, failures, and hurts. The turning point can't come until we're truly desperate enough to TURN and go in a new direction.

You may be saying, "David, I really *want* a New Beginning, but I'm troubled with past sins and failures, and with the hurts and heartaches I've suffered." If the devil is taunting you with such things, I have great news for you: God can get you out of the enemy's pigpen of failure and despair!

Look at these encouraging promises from the book of Isaiah:

> *Behold, the former things have come to pass,*
> *Now I declare new things;*
> *Before they spring forth I proclaim them to you.*
> *Sing to the LORD a new song,*
> *Sing His praise from the end of the earth!*
> (Isaiah 42:9-10)

> *Do not call to mind the former things,*
> *Or ponder things of the past.*
> *Behold, I will do something new,*
> *Now it will spring forth;*
> *Will you not be aware of it?*
> *I will even make a roadway in the wilderness,*
> *Rivers in the desert* (Isaiah 43:18-19).

Some powerful principles are contained in these brief passages of Scripture:

1. God declares His desire to give us His New Beginnings.

2. He desires to give us a *"new song,"* so we can *"sing His praises from the end of the earth."*

3. He wants to stir our hearts to be *"aware"* of the new things He's doing in our lives.

4. We are told not to *"call to mind"* or *"ponder things of the past."*

5. No matter what kinds of difficult seasons we've been facing, God wants to *"make a roadway in the wilderness, rivers in the desert."*

I encourage you to spend some time meditating on these wonderful promises from God. Instead of the devil's *pigpen,* He wants to show you His *purpose* and *provision.*

LEAVE YOUR PAST BEHIND

The apostle Paul challenges us to turn our back on the past:

One thing I do: Forgetting what is behind and straining toward what is ahead (Philippians 3:13).

You have several important reasons to forget the past:

- God has told you to leave it behind.

- You cannot change any part of it.

- If you've asked God to forgive you and give you a New Beginning, your past sins are forgotten.

- God tells you to forgive anyone who has sinned against you, because you can't be fully released from your past until you release others.

Why worry or fret over something you cannot possibly control? Your past is finished, and there's nothing you can do to resurrect it. So bury it and let it stay dead!

When you repent of your sins, forgive others, and ask for a New Beginning, God forgives and forgets your past misdeeds. Look at what the prophet Micah says about how God handles your sins and your past:

Who is a God like You, who pardons iniquity
And passes over the rebellious act of the remnant of
His possession?
He does not retain His anger forever,
Because He delights in unchanging love.

He will again have compassion on us;
He will tread our iniquities under foot.
Yes, You will cast all their sins
Into the depths of the sea (Micah 7:18-19).

When the Lord forgives you, the Bible says He buries your sins in the deepest part of the ocean! As someone has suggested, God then hangs a "No Fishing" sign to keep us from resurrecting those things ever again.

And notice the word *"all"*: *"You will cast ALL their sins into the depths of sea."* Not one of your sins is so terrible that it's unforgivable. ALL of your sins were included when you asked Jesus Christ to come into your life…when you asked Him to forgive your sins and make you a child of God.

KING DAVID'S NEW BEGINNING

Like Micah, David declares that God *"pardons ALL your iniquities"* (Psalm 103:3). At one point in his life, David was under a cloud of shame after committing adultery and murder. He cried out to God for a New Beginning:

Create in me a clean heart, O God,
And renew a steadfast spirit within me.
Do not cast me away from Your presence
And do not take Your Holy Spirit from me.
Restore to me the joy of Your salvation

And sustain me with a willing spirit (Psalm 51:10-12).

God heard David's prayer—and He will hear *yours* as well. No matter what kind of pit you have dug for yourself, the Lord can forgive you and give you a fresh start.

How fantastic it is to go from a life of sin and death to a life of joy and peace! David testified of God's amazing grace:

> *How blessed is he whose transgression is forgiven,*
> *Whose sin is covered!*
> *How blessed is the man to whom the LORD does not*
> *   impute iniquity,*
> *And in whose spirit there is no deceit! ...*
>
> *I acknowledged my sin to You,*
> *And my iniquity I did not hide;*
> *I said, "I will confess my transgressions to the LORD";*
> *And You forgave the guilt of my sin* (Psalm 32:1-5).
>
> *As far as the east is from the west,*
> *So far has He removed our transgressions from us*
> (Psalm 103:12).

Your past sins—ALL of them—have been covered by the blood of Jesus. It's time to forget them and leave them in the past, so your New Beginning can start.

FORGET YOUR SUCCESSES TOO

It's not just the sins, faults, failures, and hurts of the past that we need to forget if we are going to discover a New Beginning. Sometimes we also must forget our past successes. It may surprise you that we're supposed to forget the "glory days" of our past, but it's true!

I've known ministers who totally missed a greater day of anointing and fruitfulness simply because they were caught up in the victories of yesteryear. It's not what the Lord did 50 or 20 or 10 or even 5 years ago that we need to be concentrating on, but what He's doing NOW!

Let me share two exciting stories regarding men of God who refused to rest on the laurels of their past successes...

Dr. Charles Blair, a very dear friend of mine and of Inspiration Ministries, retired after 51 years as senior pastor of Calvary Temple Church in Denver, Colorado. When he first accepted the pastorate of the church, it was small and struggling, but under his strong leadership it became one of the premier churches in the world. Dr. Blair's powerful ministry not only impacted Denver, but his passion for missions brought a harvest of thousands of souls in other nations as well.

When Dr. Blair retired as pastor, he thought he would spend his twilight years writing his memoirs and taking life easier. However, God had a different plan in mind for him— a plan much bigger than Dr. Blair ever imagined.

God's plan for his later years would dwarf anything Dr. Blair had done in the past 51 years of ministry. The Lord challenged him to do the impossible...to plant 1,000 churches in Ethiopia in two years.

When this challenge came to him, Dr. Blair had already passed his 81st birthday, well past the time that most men and women decide to withdraw from the battlefront of ministry and concentrate on their grandchildren and great-grandchildren. Not so with this stalwart man of faith. Like Caleb of Old Testament fame, Charles Blair accepted God's challenge and embarked on an exciting New Beginning. Rather than *retire*, he chose to *re-fire*.

MY DAD'S NEW BEGINNINGS

Another man of unshakeable faith, boundless energy, and passion for ministry is my father, Dr. Morris Cerullo. Many of Dad's contemporaries have long since embraced retirement, choosing to leave the Great Commission to the younger generation. But Dad continues to circle the globe and preach the Gospel of Jesus Christ.

I'm proud of how my father has preached to multitudes in more than 133 countries, often meeting and praying with kings, presidents, prime ministers, and rulers in the nations of the world. He has battled the forces of darkness in places such as India, Africa, Colombia, Argentina, Brazil, Mexico, the Philippines, and the Middle East. Many of the nations, such as Saudi Arabia, Kuwait, Egypt, and Jordan are countries that forbid the preaching of the Gospel. Yet God has opened amazing doors in these countries for my dad to minister God's love and miracle-working power to the lost.

My dad is younger at age 75 than many men half his age. One of his secrets is simply that he refuses to rest on past laurels. Rather than looking at old endings, Dad is constantly looking for New Beginnings!

Don't think that my father or Dr. Blair have always had an easy or glamorous life. They have each experienced their share of storms and winter seasons—but they've chosen to see rainbows rather than clouds. They are heroes of the faith who look for New Beginnings from God every day!

 ## *Searching Your Heart*

1. Read the story of the Prodigal Son in Luke 15. The word "prodigal" means "wasteful or recklessly extravagant." Reflect on the ways in which you have wasted your life or been reckless with God's gifts to you.

2. God wants to give you a New Beginning. In order to receive this gift from Him, what are the sins and failures of your past that you need to leave behind? Ask Him to reveal these to you. Make a list of them now.

3. Write down your past successes that you are proud of. Consider if there is any way that these past achievements could actually be holding you back from receiving your New Beginning from God.

4. Spend time with God now, talking with Him about your past failures.

   - Worship Him that a New Beginning is possible because of His mercy and grace toward you.

   - Repent for any sins and failures of the past He has revealed to you.

   - Ask Him to cover your past with the blood of Jesus and to fill you again with the power of His Holy Spirit so you can live in freedom from these snares in the future.

REMEMBER THE 'THREE-LEGGED STOOL'

YOUR NEW BEGINNING NEEDS a proper spiritual foundation, and this can best be illustrated by thinking about a simple three-legged footstool. Take away just one of those legs, and you will fall over if you attempt to sit on the stool. Take away two of the legs, and the best you can hope for is to somehow balance yourself against the remaining leg so you don't fall. And with all three legs gone, you soon will be flat on the floor, wondering what happened!

In the same way, many Christians today are missing one or more "legs" in their spiritual "footstool," yet they wonder why they struggle to remain upright. They may even try to decorate or paint their footstool to improve its appearance, but the result will still be dismal unless all three legs are intact.

What are the three vital legs that we need in our spiritual lives? Although many important ingredients could be listed for a fruitful Christian life, these three are absolutely essential:

1. Praise and Worship

2. The Word of God

3. Prayer

If all three of these are in proper operation in your life, you will be spiritually strong and balanced, able to deal with the fiery darts Satan throws at you in the circumstances of life. But take away even ONE of these essential spiritual "legs," and you soon will find yourself faltering!

EMBRACE THE FUNDAMENTALS

Many Believers are searching for some "deep" truth to make them more spiritual, when their real problem is a failure to do the fundamental disciplines of the Christian life. While this three-legged stool illustration may seem simplistic to some of the "deeper life" folks, the tragedy is that many have skipped over these essential foundations for growth.

Vince Lombardi was one of the greatest NFL football coaches of all time. He brought the Green Bay Packers to several championships, and his teams were always known for their careful execution of the fundamentals of the game.

Although Lombardi was coaching some of the best athletes in the world, he always took time to reinforce the importance of the fundamentals. He was known on more than one occasion in the locker room to pick up a ball and say to his players, "Men, this is a football."

Some of the new players probably thought their coach was crazy. "What's wrong with this guy?" they may have asked each other. "Doesn't he realize that we already know everything there is to know about football? After all, we've been playing the game since we were kids!"

But Lombardi had a very important message for his team—a message we also would do well to heed. In essence, he was saying, "Men, no matter how skilled or talented you think you are, it's time to get back to the basics. We'll win games not by being clever or complicated, but by concentrating on the fundamentals."

So I encourage you today—whether you've been a Christian for a long time or are just in the process of exploring a relationship with Christ—take time to learn how to do the basics...take time for the three-legged stool.

INTIMACY WITH GOD

Embracing the three-legged stool will help you experience new spiritual strength, a more intimate relationship with the Lord, and a powerful new sense of God's presence and purpose.

Although it's hard for me to believe, pollsters report that more than 33% of today's Christians claim they have never felt the presence of God. An even higher percentage claim they have never heard God speak to them in any way, shape, or form.

This is not the kind of relationship God wants with you! Our Heavenly Father doesn't just want you to know *about* Him, He wants you to know **HIM**! Jesus promised, *"My sheep hear My voice"* (John 10:27).

God designed us to experience an intimate relationship with Him. In the book of Genesis, we read about how God walked with Adam and Eve in the Garden of Eden in the cool of the day, interacting and speaking face to face with them (Genesis 3:8). Until Adam and Eve sinned, they enjoyed sweet, harmonious fellowship with the Lord each day.

In 1913, Austin Miles wrote a song that describes the wonderful, intimate relationship God wants to have with His children. The chorus of "In the Garden" says:

And He walks with me and He talks with me,
And He tells me I am His own.
And the joys we share as we tarry there,
None other has ever known.

What an incredible picture of the kind of fellowship God wants to have with each one of us. Staying seated on the three-legged stool at the foot of His throne will further that kind of intimacy, making us spiritually strong, stable, and victorious in our Christian life.

BEGIN WITH PRAISE AND WORSHIP

The first leg of the stool is praise and worship, as we are told in Psalm 100:4: *"Enter His gates with thanksgiving and His courts with praise."* Thanksgiving and praise are our *entry point* into God's presence!

Why is it so important to come into the presence of God through praise and worship? Because only in God's presence will you truly change...only in His presence will you find strength to overcome the attacks of the enemy.

Paul describes the path to transformation this way:

> *Now the Lord is the Spirit, and where the Spirit of the Lord is, there is liberty. But we all, with unveiled face, beholding as in a mirror the glory of the Lord, are being transformed into the same image from glory to glory, just as from the Lord, the Spirit* (2 Corinthians 3:17-18).

Everything you need can be found in God's presence! Whether you need a physical healing...financial break-throughs...freedom from fear, depression, and anxiety...or the restoration of a relationship with a loved one—your life and circumstances can be transformed in an instant!

Jacob experienced a powerful encounter with God's presence (Genesis 32:24-31). After spending time wrestling with Him, Jacob's name was changed...his walk was changed...his outlook was changed…and even his DESTINY was changed! Instead of merely *seeking* the "Blessing," Jacob *became* a blessing!

DEFINING MOMENTS

Never underestimate the power of **one moment** in God's presence. That's where you will find your New Beginning, and it's where you will be empowered to overcome the devil and fulfill God's purpose for your life.

King Jehoshaphat once faced seemingly insurmountable enemies, but the Lord told him, *"Don't be afraid…the battle is not yours, but **Mine**"* (2 Chronicles 20:15). So how did God instruct Jehoshaphat to win the battle? Through praise and worship!

> *He appointed those who sang to the LORD and those who praised Him in holy attire, as they went out before the army and said, "Give thanks to the LORD, for His lovingkindness is everlasting." When they began singing and praising, **the LORD set ambushes against the sons of Ammon, Moab and Mount Seir, who had come against Judah; so they were **routed*** (2 Chronicles 20:21-22).

Just as King Jehoshaphat learned, God can use our praise and worship as a powerful weapon to rout our spiritual enemies and give us overwhelming victory!

Praising and worshipping God causes us to surrender all the things in our life that have brought us fear…frustration…anxiety…confusion…and pain. Through praise and worship, we recognize that **He alone** is able to solve our problems and transform our lives.

Worship lifts us UP and OUT of the things of this world

and places us in the realm of God's Spirit. There the Lord showers us with His mercy, love, and grace, and He confirms that HE'S IN CONTROL of *everything*!

What a wonderful experience and privilege it is to step out of our earthly cares and into the supernatural presence and provision of Almighty God!

But we still need two more legs on our footstool...

 *Searching Your Heart*

1. What are the three foundational "legs" of your spiritual "footstool"?

2. Why is intimacy with God so important? On a scale of 1-10, with 1 indicating absolutely *no* intimacy with God and 10 representing a powerfully intimate relationship, rate your current intimacy level with the Lord.

3. God wants to fill you with His presence, His power, and His peace. Regardless of where you are in your relationship with Him, He wants to be so much closer to you. How does this make you feel? What do you truly desire to have changed in your relationship with God? Record your thoughts now.

4. Spend time talking with God now about your relationship with Him.

   ▪ Thank Him that He desires to be close to you.

   ▪ Tell Him how you feel about all this, and ask Him to give you the desire for an increasingly intimate relationship with Him.

   ▪ Focus now on the spiritual "leg" of praise and worship. Turn to Psalm 27 and use this as a prayer to pray to Him. If you have a favorite hymn or worship chorus, sing it to Him. If not, you can sing a new song to Him using your own words to express your love and adoration.

   Note: Because most of us are uncomfortable worshipping God freely, your private praise and worship may make you feel a bit uncomfortable at first. But the more you spend time praising and worshipping the Lord, the easier it will become to honor and adore Him with both the thoughts of your heart *and* the words of your mouth.

EAT *Your* DAILY BREAD

EVERY DAY, WE NEED TO TAKE TIME for each of the three legs of our spiritual stool—entering God's presence to worship, studying His Word, and praying. Jesus taught us to pray, *"Give us this day our DAILY bread"* (Matthew 6:11).

When the children of Israel received manna in the wilderness, it never lasted for more than a day. God gave them enough for that day, but by the next day the manna was rotten:

> *Then the LORD said to Moses, "Behold, I will rain bread from heaven for you; and the people shall go out and **gather a day's portion every day**, that I may test them, whether or not they will walk in My instruction"* (Exodus 16:4).

> *But they did not listen to Moses, and some left part of it until morning, and it **bred worms** and became **foul**; and Moses was angry with them* (Exodus 16:20).

Did you ever wonder why the children of Israel couldn't collect enough manna for a month or even a week? The answer is simple: God wanted to teach them—and *us*—a valuable spiritual lesson. Instead of being dependent on our own strength and resources, He wants us to be dependent on **Him** to meet our needs on a *daily* basis!

ARE YOU STARVING SPIRITUALLY?

My dad often says, "All truth is parallel." No one could survive in the natural world if they only ate once a week or once a month. Before long they would be dead. Yet many of God's children today are starving to death spiritually, and they don't even recognize it! They are spiritually weak and powerless because they have gone for days…weeks…months…or even years without spending quality time to nourish their lives with the Word of God!

Jesus warned, *"Man shall not live by bread alone but by every word* [the written Word and the Living Word] *that proceeds out of the mouth of God"* (Matthew 4:4). Unless we regularly partake of this spiritual food, our New Beginning will be malnourished and our relationship with God will wither.

Jesus said of Himself, *"I am the bread of life"* (John 6:35). As we study the Bible, we need to keep in mind that it's all about a RELATIONSHIP with God—not just the accumulation of religious facts about Him.

That's why Jesus challenged the religious leaders that they were missing the point when they studied the Scriptures: *"You search the Scriptures because you think that in them you have eternal life; it is these that testify about Me; and you are unwilling to come to Me so that you may have life"* (John 5:39-40).

AMAZING BENEFITS OF GOD'S WORD

The Word of God is the second leg of our spiritual footstool…a crucial part of our foundation…and important fuel for our New Beginning.

God gives us so many wonderful promises about the power of reading, studying, meditating on, and obeying His Word:

- **Nourishment.** The Bible is food that nourishes our spiritual life. Hebrews 5:12-14 describes the teachings of God's Word as both milk and solid food—providing the spiritual nutrients we need in order to grow.

- **Cleansing.** God's Word renews our minds and cleanses our hearts (Romans 12:2, Ephesians 5:26).

- **Guidance.** God's Word shines a light on our pathway and shows us the right way to go! David says in Psalm 119:105, *"Your word is a lamp to my feet and a light to my path."*

- **Strength and security.** God's Word gives us strength for the day...strength to overcome the trials, tests, and difficult circumstances that come our way! Jesus tells us:

   Everyone who comes to Me and hears My words and acts on them...is like a man building a house, who dug deep and laid a foundation on the rock; and when a flood occurred, the torrent burst against that house and could not shake it, because it had been well built (Luke 6:47-48).

- **Fruitfulness.** God promises success and spiritual fruitfulness to those who meditate on His Word and obey it (Joshua 1:8, Psalm 1:1-3).

- **Victory.** God's Word alerts us to Satan's schemes, and it serves as a two-edged sword to defeat him (2 Corinthians 2:11, Hebrews 4:12, Ephesians 6:17). When the devil came in the wilderness to tempt Jesus, it was the Word of God that Jesus used to overcome the attack. Jesus said to him: *"It is written...It is written...It is written!"* (Matthew 4:1-11)

EXAMINING YOUR LIFE

In light of these fantastic promises, I encourage you to pause and do an honest assessment of whether your life is truly founded upon God's Word. Can you honestly say you're walking in the blessings God offers to those who study and obey His Word? If not, ask Him to show you any areas where you need a New Beginning of *obedience*...so He can give you a New Beginning of *blessing!*

As you prepare to embark on your New Beginning with God, ask yourself these questions:

1. Do you know the blessings and promises that are yours as a child of God?

2. Do you know how to come into a Covenant Relationship with God, so you're able to walk under His protection and provision every day of your life?

3. Is your life controlled by God's Word more than by your feelings?

4. Does God's Word shape your confidence in the future, or is your perspective swayed by your present circumstances?

START YOUR NEW HABITS TODAY!

How did your spiritual assessment go as you answered the above questions? My purpose in pressing these issues isn't to make you feel ashamed or guilty. I simply want you to see God's heart to draw you closer and closer into an intimate relationship with Him—through worship, the Word, and prayer.

If you don't already have a daily habit of devotion to the

three legs of your spiritual stool, then it's crucial for you to stop what you're doing and answer these questions:

- What time and place are best for my daily appointment with God?

- What are some specific ways I can bolster each leg of my spiritual stool—worship, the Word, and prayer?

Once you've considered these questions, I encourage you to take a few minutes and write down what you've concluded. This will help you go from "wishful thinking" to a firm commitment to grow stronger in the Lord.

And you will also want to learn more about *prayer*—the third leg of your spiritual stool…

 *Searching Your Heart*

1. How would you describe your diet of "daily bread" from God's Word? Are you stuffed full? Hungry for more? Malnourished? Starving to death?

2. Does God's Word shape your confidence in the future, or is your perspective swayed by your present circumstances? Why?

3. Review the list in this chapter of God's promises for those who choose to faithfully "eat" His Word. Write down how you see yourself benefiting in your personal life from each of these six promises.

4. Spend time talking with God now about your New Beginning with His Word.

   ▪ Thank God for His Word. Agree with Him that it will provide nourishment, cleansing, guidance, and victory in your life.

   ▪ Ask Him to show you how you can improve your daily habits regarding His Word. Make a commitment to Him that you will make these changes.

   ▪ If your life is controlled more by your feelings than by God's Word, confess this sin to Him now. Ask Him to give you a craving to eat the Bread of His Word every day.

PRAYER: THE FOOTSTOOL'S THIRD LEG

THE THIRD LEG OF YOUR "SPIRITUAL STOOL" is prayer. This is an indispensable key to a Believer's power for living, yet it's sorely lacking in the lives of many of God's people today.

There's a common misconception that we only need to pray when we have a specific need. Yes, God does welcome our prayers in our times of trouble, but that's only a small part of His purpose in giving us the privilege of prayer.

Instead of merely engaging in "crisis prayers," the Lord wants us to develop a prayer life of daily communion and fellowship with Him. Without having this open and honest communication on a daily basis, we will end up knowing ABOUT God...without truly knowing *HIM*!

In Psalm 32:6, David says to the Lord: *"Let everyone who is godly pray to You in a time when You may be found. Surely in a flood of great waters they will not reach him."*

The clear message in David's prayer is that you shouldn't wait until the storm hits before you start praying! Make sure you have a strong spiritual foundation *before* the flood waters arrive at your door (Matthew 7:24-27)!

YOU ARE CALLED TO PRAY!

Not everyone is called to be a preacher or a missionary in

foreign lands, but *everyone* is called to pray! For a Christian, praying is as natural and as essential as breathing is for our physical bodies.

The Bible gives countless promises about the power God has given us through prayer. James 5:16 tells us that *"the effectual fervent prayer of a righteous man accomplishes much."*

So why is it that many Christians neglect the kind of regular, disciplined prayer life that God calls us to? Although we could list many reasons, I believe the primary ones are *unbelief* and *laziness.*

Jesus clearly links *answered* prayer to *believing* prayer:

> *Jesus answered saying to them, "Have faith in God.*
> *Truly I say to you, whoever says to this mountain, 'Be*
> *taken up and cast into the sea,' and does not doubt in*
> *his heart, but believes that what he says is going to*
> *happen, it will be granted him. Therefore I say to you,*
> *all things for which you pray and ask, believe that you*
> *have received them, and they will be granted you"*
> (Mark 11:22-24).

When we truly pray in faith, we "see" the answer to our prayer even before it actually arrives. As Jesus tells us in Matthew 19:26, *"All things are possible with God!"*

James, likewise, encourages Believers to *"ask in faith without any doubting,"* for the person who doubts *"ought not to expect that he will receive anything from the Lord"* (James 1:6-7).

God wants you to believe His promises when you pray!

THE DISCIPLINE OF PRAYER

Although prayer should come naturally to a person who has been born again by God's Spirit, it also requires WORK.

The three legs of your spiritual stool are "spiritual disciplines" that require consistency and persistence.

Despite the wonderful promises the Bible gives us about prayer, many Believers are simply unwilling to engage in the hard work required for a successful prayer life. Look at these quotes from some men of God who challenged Christians to be more devoted to prayer:

> *"Spiritual work is taxing work, and men are loath to do it. Praying, true praying, costs an outlay of serious attention and of time, which flesh and blood do not relish."* – E.M. Bounds

> *"The great people of the earth today are the people who pray. I do not mean those who talk about prayer; nor those who say they believe in prayer; nor yet those who can explain about prayer; but I mean those people who take time to pray."* – S.D. Gordon

Are you willing to sacrifice a portion of your time to meet with God each day? This is a vital key to a powerful Christian life! It unlocks the treasure chest of God's wisdom…His guidance…His presence…His power…and His blessings!

GO DEEPER IN YOUR PRAYER LIFE

Many Christians are satisfied with only praying in church on Sundays and saying "grace" at the dinner table. If this pretty much describes your prayer life, God wants to take you deeper!

Of course, the devil will fight you on this each step of the way. He knows the awesome power you have in Jesus' name! If the enemy can discourage you from praying, he has neutralized much of your effectiveness as a warrior for God's Kingdom. You become like a soldier who has been stripped of his weapons and rendered powerless.

Don't let the devil or the busyness of life distract you from a powerful, daily time of prayer! Find a set time of day or night when you can be alone with God without the concerns of the day whirling around in your mind. For some, this may be the first thing in the morning. For others, it may be the last thing before going to bed. The key is to make a daily appointment to meet with God!

You may think you don't have the time or energy to pray, but I have found the opposite to be true. It's when I miss my special time of prayer that I feel overwhelmed, fatigued, and under greater attacks from the devil! But after my prayer time, I sense clearer direction from God, renewed energy, and a sense of greater protection from the enemy.

God wants to take your prayer life deeper than the "Now I lay me down to sleep" bedtime rhyme. He wants you to experience the kind of prayer that defeats the devil, heals the sick, raises the dead, restores broken marriages, destroys addictions, delivers the downtrodden, sets the captives free, and glorifies the Lord!

This kind of prayer life is not wimpy, half-hearted, wishy-washy, or apologetic. It's as bold as a lion, bright as the sun, strong as an ox, and as stable as a mountain. It refuses to give up or back down in the face of adversity.

The Lord wants to bring you into a prayer life that's a delight rather than a drudgery. Instead of the mindless recitation of religious mumbo jumbo, He wants you to experience intimate, heart-to-heart fellowship with Him—the One who is the Lover of your soul and the Ruler of the universe.

GIVE GOD YOUR TIME

Just as it takes time to build a human relationship, Heaven-moving, earth-shaking, hell-defeating prayer requires a commitment of your time. Too many people treat prayer as if God is operating a McPrayer drive-through service where they can place an order, pick it up 10 seconds later, and keep on driving down the road. It doesn't work that way.

Do you really want an intimate relationship with God? There are no shortcuts! The way to get to know Him and experience His power is to spend time in His presence. This comes through praise and worship, reading His Word, and talking with Him in prayer.

Think about it… You can't get to know someone by merely *hearing about* him or her. Getting to know someone requires talking in depth with them. You must spend TIME with them.

Kids today spell love T-I-M-E. "If you really love me," they say, "you'll spend time with me." It's exactly the same in our relationship with God. If you want to demonstrate your love for Him…if you truly want to get to know Him…the most important thing you can do is spend time with Him.

PERSEVERE IN YOUR PRAYERS

Many Christians have an anemic prayer life because they don't understand the need for persistence in their prayers. In Luke 18, Jesus tells the story of a widow who is trying to get justice from an unjust judge. He isn't at all inclined to help her, but eventually she wears him down by her persistence.

God is NOT an unjust Judge—He's your loving Heavenly Father. However, Jesus tells this story because He wants us to learn the importance of perseverance in our prayers. Don't give up if your prayers aren't immediately answered!

The prophet Daniel once prayed for 20 days with no answer. Still he believed God and persisted in his prayers. Perhaps Daniel felt discouraged at times or bewildered about why God seemingly hadn't responded to his prayers, yet he didn't give up!

Finally, Daniel's answer came on the 21st day. His persistence and time seeking God were rewarded!

PUSH...PRAY UNTIL SOMETHING HAPPENS!

While Daniel spent many days praying for God's intervention, some of you may have been praying for many *years* that God's will be done in a particular situation. Sometimes this has to do with the needs of our children or grandchildren or our husband or wife.

I once heard a story about a rebellious young boy who was causing his mom a lot of trouble. She sent him to a Christian camp in hopes that he would meet the Lord there. God's Spirit was really moving during one of the fireside services, and the boy ran out into the woods because he was determined not to be touched by the Lord.

The boy yelled up at the heavens, "Why won't You just leave me alone?" and he heard a voice say from above, "Then tell your mother to leave *Me* alone."

Your children need to know they won't be able to escape from the Lord, because you're constantly banging on Heaven's door on their behalf. Your children may be straying from God's purposes at the moment, but sooner or later God will pierce their hearts. Persevere. Be persistent in your prayers. Your answer will come.

Barbara and I spent so many nights praying for our son Ben when he had moved away from home and was far from God. Often as we prayed, we would worship and thank the Lord as if Ben's heart had already been changed—and soon it was! Today he has a powerful youth ministry called Steelroots, which is reaching hundreds of thousands of teens around the world. Our once-wayward son was recently named by a leading Christian magazine as one of the Top 30 Youth Ministers in the nation!

When Jesus tells us to ask, seek, and knock in Matthew 7:7, the verb tense in the original Greek could actually be better translated:

> Ask...and keep on asking
> Seek...and keep on seeking
> Knock...and keep on knocking

This means our prayers are supposed to be *persistent* and *persevering*. It's the **PUSH** principle: <u>P</u>ray <u>U</u>ntil <u>S</u>omething <u>H</u>appens! Don't give up until the answer comes!

If you take time for all three legs of the "three-legged stool," I guarantee that you won't be disappointed. Praise and worship, God's Word, and prayer are the "Miracle Grow" required to nourish your New Beginning!

 *Searching Your Heart*

1. Why is prayer a spiritual discipline we need to practice each day?

2. Write about a time when you applied the **PUSH** principle to a situation in your life or in the life of a loved one. What were the results when you <u>P</u>rayed <u>U</u>ntil <u>S</u>omething <u>H</u>appened?

3. Describe your past and current practice of daily prayer. What changes can you make to improve your prayer life?

4. Spend time now talking with God about your prayer life.

   - Praise Him that He's inviting you to go deeper with Him in prayer.

   - Ask Him to forgive you for any ways you've neglected this vital leg of your three-legged footstool.

   - Make a plan with the Lord for how you will consistently pursue a more intimate prayer life with Him.

BEGIN AGAIN THROUGH FELLOWSHIP

EACH OF THE ELEMENTS OF THE "three-legged stool" is meant to bring you into a stronger and more intimate relationship with God. Nothing is more important than these in helping you grow in your New Beginning.

However, the relationships you have with PEOPLE are also important to the success of your Christian life. When more than 3,000 people were saved after Peter preached on the day of Pentecost, one of the first things these new converts did was to find fellowship with other Believers:

> They were continually **devoting themselves** to the apostles' teaching and to **fellowship**, to the breaking of bread and to prayer...

> Day by day continuing with one mind in the temple, and breaking bread from house to house, they were taking their meals together with gladness and sincerity of heart (Acts 2:42, 46).

The word *"fellowship"* is the Greek word *koinonia*, which means to have something in common, to share, or to have communion with each other. Those who are walking in fellowship with Christ are meant to share that relationship with other Believers:

What we have seen and heard we proclaim to you also,
*so that you too may have **fellowship** with us; and*
*indeed our **fellowship** is with the Father, and with His*
Son Jesus Christ.

...if we walk in the Light as He Himself is in the
*Light, we have **fellowship** with one another, and*
the blood of Jesus His Son cleanses us from all sin
(1 John 1:3, 7).

What a beautiful principle this is: Those who have fellowship with the Lord are supposed to find other Christians to walk together with in this life. As you start your New Beginning with God, remember that the Lord wants to put people in your life who can strengthen, equip, and support you.

WHY DO WE NEED FELLOWSHIP?

Some independent-minded folks might question the value of fellowship with other Christians. "David, isn't my relationship with God all I need?" they ask. "The 'three-legged stool' is helping me grow in my intimacy with the Lord, but I don't really see why fellowship with people is important."

Take a look at what God's Word says about this:

Let us consider how to stimulate one another to love
and good deeds, not forsaking our own assembling
together, as is the habit of some, but encouraging one
another; and all the more as you see the day drawing
near (Hebrews 10:24-25).

God tells us in this passage that we need other Christians in our life to *"stimulate"* us *"to love and good deeds."* Just as hot coals on a barbecue grill will soon grow cold if they are separated from the other coals, the enemy wants to sow offenses among Believers so they will lose this vital connection with each other.

No matter how strong we feel in our relationship with God, there will be times when we need the encouragement and support of other Christians. In fact, the Bible tells us to encourage each other on a *daily* basis:

> *Take care, brethren, that there not be in any one of you an evil, unbelieving heart that falls away from the living God. But encourage one another day after day, as long as it is still called "Today," so that none of you will be hardened by the deceitfulness of sin* (Hebrews 3:12-13).

More than 30 times in the New Testament, we are told to do something together with *"one another."* We are to love one another, serve one another, honor one another, bear one another's burdens, pray for one another...and the list goes on. The normal Christian life isn't something for Lone Rangers— God meant for us to have other Christians to walk with on the journey of faith.

A SOBER WARNING

Just as Godly Christian friends can be a tremendous encouragement to your New Beginning, nothing can sabotage your New Beginning faster than hanging out with people who are toxic, unbelieving, dishonest, or immoral. As one old preacher admonished his church, "If you sleep with dogs, you'll wake up with fleas!"

The apostle Paul warns, *"Do not be deceived: 'Bad company corrupts good morals'"* (1 Corinthians 15:33). Note that Satan often uses *"bad company"* to *deceive* us. Toxic friends are not likely to *tell us* they want to ruin our life by exposing us to drugs...drunkenness...immorality...STDs...dishonesty...gossip...selfishness...grumbling...or breaches of the law. No, they inevitably come with a sweet siren song that lulls us to sleep and distracts our hearts from the things of God.

Often we deceive ourselves into thinking we can compromise with worldly and evil ways, while still maintaining a close relationship with God. Paul challenges the Corinthians about this:

> *Do not be bound together with unbelievers; for*
> *what partnership have righteousness and lawlessness,*
> *or what fellowship has light with darkness? Or*
> *what harmony has Christ with Belial, or what has*
> *a believer in common with an unbeliever?*
> (2 Corinthians 6:14-15)

Does this mean we shouldn't associate with any non-Christians after our New Beginning? No, in order to avoid all contact with unbelievers, we would have to be raptured and go straight to Heaven! However, Paul is saying we need to be careful about getting emotionally tangled in close relationships with people who have no intention of following God. We may think we are changing *them*, but often it's the other way around.

King Solomon puts this in perspective: *"He who walks with wise men will be wise, but the companion of fools will suffer harm"* (Proverbs 13:20). Do you want to be wise and find success in your New Beginning? Then find wise people to walk with! Harm will surely come to those who choose to be *"the companion of fools."*

Sometimes even professing Christians can be used by the enemy to distract us from God's high calling for our lives.

Perhaps they're filled with negativity and unbelief…or harbor offenses toward other Believers…or have compromised with Biblical standards of morality and integrity. Paul warns us in 1 Corinthians 5:11 to stay away from such people!

THE PATH OF BLESSING

God wants to bless you. His warning against ungodly relationships is intended to spare you from harm and keep you from any influences that will hinder your New Beginning.

Psalm 1 tells us that God's path of blessing requires the elimination of relationships that would impair our spiritual growth:

> *How blessed is the man who does not walk in the*
> *counsel of the wicked,*
> *Nor stand in the path of sinners,*
> *Nor sit in the seat of scoffers!* (Psalm 1:1)

Pause a moment and ask the Lord to search your heart in light of this passage:

- Have you been living your life according to the counsel of wicked people—whether that counsel came from personal relationships or through ungodly media influences?

- Have you allowed peer pressure to sway you to walk *"in the path of sinners"* instead of God's paths of righteousness?

- Do you hang out with people who openly mock God and scoff at the principles in His Word?

Rather than letting toxic relationships squeeze you into the world's mold, Psalm 1 encourages us to allow our lives to be shaped by obedience to God's Word:

But his delight is in the law of the LORD,
And in His law he meditates day and night.
He will be like a tree firmly planted by streams of water,
Which yields its fruit in its season
And its leaf does not wither;
And in whatever he does, he prospers (Psalm 1:2-3).

God wants your New Beginning to lead to this kind of blessed life!

- Instead of being blown about by the circumstances of life, He wants you to be *"like a tree firmly planted."*

- He wants to help you escape from the winter seasons of life, so you can *"yield fruit in its season."*

- He wants to bless and prosper your life in everything you do!

Your New Beginning is just the *beginning* of a new life of blessing in Covenant Relationship with Jesus Christ! Don't let *anything* hold you back from God's wonderful plan for your life.

 *Searching Your Heart*

1. Why do we all need good, Godly fellowship with other Believers?

2. Describe your closest relationships. Prayerfully consider whether each one is strengthening your relationship with the Lord or weakening it.

3. Reread Psalm 1:1. Considering this verse, are there any relationships in your life from which you need to distance yourself? Why?

4. Spend time now talking with God about your relationships.

   ▪ Thank Him for the healthy, Godly relationships He has given you.

   ▪ Ask Him to forgive you for any unhealthy, ungodly relationships in which you've allowed yourself to become involved.

   ▪ Now, with His help, decide which relationships you are going to separate yourself from, and how He wants you to do this. Next, focus on which relationships He wants you to work on strengthening, so you may both receive and give encouragement concerning intimacy with the Lord.

*Release your
faith by sowing
an uncommon
seed to honor
the Lord.*

BEGIN AGAIN WITH *Your* FINANCIAL SEED

HONORING THE LORD WITH YOUR FINANCES is a powerful key for releasing your faith and unlocking God's New Beginning for your life. I've received testimonies from *thousands* of Believers who discovered their New Beginning as they sowed uncommon financial seeds into God's Kingdom.

Solomon, who was probably the richest man in the world in his day, shows the amazing connection between our financial faithfulness and receiving supernatural abundance from God:

> *Honor the LORD from your wealth*
> *And from the firstfruits of all your produce;*
> *So your barns will be filled with plenty*
> *And your vats will overflow with new wine*
> (Proverbs 3:9-10).

Notice that the Bible says we are to honor the Lord with the *"firstfruits"* of our finances—not the leftovers after all our bills are paid. This kind of obedient giving requires FAITH, because we must trust God to fulfill His promise to bless those who honor Him with their wealth.

If you've been living paycheck to paycheck and struggling just to have enough to pay your bills, remember God's desire to give you *more than enough*. He wants your life to *"overflow"* with His blessings!

This principle is a reflection of God's Covenant Relationship with you as His child: When you give God your resources, He promises to give you *His* resources. This is a GREAT EXCHANGE, isn't it? Giving is part of God's divine nature, and when His nature gets in you, you'll want to give back to Him!

YOU CAN'T OUT-GIVE GOD

Jesus tells us:

Give, and it will be given to you. They will pour into your lap a good measure—pressed down, shaken together, and running over. For by your standard of measure it will be measured to you in return (Luke 6:38).

What an incredible promise! As one preacher points out, "We give to God with teaspoons, but He returns it to us in 50-gallon barrels!"

Since the world began, no one has been able to out-give God. He's the owner of the entire universe, and He has an unlimited supply of resources. Paul points out that *"from Him and through Him and to Him are all things"* (Romans 11:36). James, likewise, says, *"Every good thing given and every perfect gift is from above, coming down from the Father of lights, with whom there is no variation or shifting shadow"* (James 1:17).

God owns it all, and when you're in a Covenant Relationship with Him, you own it all too! The Bible even teaches that God is the One who supplies us with the seeds to plant— so we can reap a great harvest!

Now He who supplies seed to the sower and bread for food will supply and multiply your seed for sowing

*and increase the harvest of your righteousness; you
will be **enriched in everything** for all liberality, which
through us is producing thanksgiving to God*
(2 Corinthians 9:10-11).

This passage doesn't say God provides seeds to *everyone*—
it says He supplies those who are *sowers!* So the best way to
receive a financial breakthrough from God is to set your heart
on sowing financial seeds into His Kingdom.

But the promise in this Scripture passage isn't limited to
finances. It says that faithful sowers will be *"enriched in EVERY-
THING."* Isn't that awesome? Whatever your need is today—
whether financial pressures, a broken relationship, an illness, an
addiction, or problems on your job—God will miraculously
step into your circumstances when you sow your seed!

Whether you need a New Beginning in your finances or
some other area of your life today, I encourage you to release
your faith by sowing an uncommon seed to honor the Lord.

SOWING SEEDS IN DIFFICULT TIMES

As hard as it may be, one of the most powerful ways to
find victory in your winter season is to sow generous financial
seeds. This is something my wife Barbara and I have often
done in our lives. When we've had a big need, we've sown a
big seed. God has done amazing things in response to these
simple acts of faith and obedience.

There are numerous examples in Scripture where people
made an offering to God in hopes that their seed...their offering...would move the Lord to act on their behalf and respond
to their need. I especially love the story about how Isaac
sowed in a time of drought and famine:

Now there was a famine in the land...

Now Isaac sowed in that land and reaped in the same year a hundredfold. And the LORD blessed him, and the man became rich, and continued to grow richer until he became very wealthy; for he had possessions of flocks and herds and a great household, so that the Philistines envied him (Genesis 26:1,12-14).

I don't know about you, but many people are tempted to *hoard* their seeds during times of insecurity and lack. But not Isaac! He chose to trust God and sow seeds in the Promised Land! And the Lord rewarded him with a gigantic harvest that was the envy of everyone around.

Remember: You are a walking warehouse of seed. Everything you have is either *enough*...your harvest...or it's the seed you need to produce your *more-than-enough* harvest. I encourage you to follow Isaac's example and sow seeds even in your difficult seasons of life.

A WIDOW'S HARVEST

I also love the story of God's supernatural provision for the prophet Elijah during a time of drought. Originally, the Lord provided for Elijah at the brook Cherith, where ravens brought him bread and meat twice a day. But when the brook dried up, God told Elijah:

Arise, go to Zarephath, which belongs to Sidon, and stay there; behold, I have commanded a widow there to provide for you (1 Kings 17:9).

When Elijah received this word from God, he must have thought, "This is wonderful. The Lord is sending me to a rich widow who has plenty of food and resources to provide for me." However, when he found the widow, she and her son were one meal away from starving to death! She was stuck in a "winter season" that seemed totally hopeless.

When Elijah asked this impoverished widow for a piece of bread, she replied:

> *As the LORD your God lives, I have no bread, only a handful of flour in the bowl and a little oil in the jar; and behold, I am gathering a few sticks that I may go in and prepare for me and my son, that we may eat it and die* (v. 12).

At this point, Elijah might have thought, "Wow. Maybe this isn't the correct widow! I surely can't ask *her* for anything, when she and her son are destitute." But the prophet of God didn't back down from his request:

> *Do not fear; go, do as you have said, but make me a little bread cake from it first and bring it out to me, and afterward you may make one for yourself and for your son. For thus says the LORD God of Israel, "The bowl of flour shall not be exhausted, nor shall the jar of oil be empty, until the day that the LORD sends rain on the face of the earth"* (vs. 13-14).

The widow must have wondered if this guy was crazy. However, since she was going to die anyway unless God did a miracle, her desperation overcame any skepticism:

> *So she went and did according to the word of Elijah, and she and he and her household ate for many days. The bowl of flour was not exhausted nor did the jar of oil become empty, according to the word of the LORD which He spoke through Elijah* (vs. 15-16).

What a great example of someone who sowed a seed during a time of incredible lack! As a result, the widow miraculously received a New Beginning of prosperity and blessing. She and her son *"ate for many days"* on that handful of flour and small amount of oil! As this faithful woman obeyed the word from God's prophet, she and her household received a harvest of supernatural abundance.

A PLAGUE AVERTED

First Chronicles 21 tells the story of King David's sin of doing a census to determine the strength of his troops, even after he was warned that this would grieve the Lord. God was angry at this and gave David the choice of three different consequences for his transgression. Each of these proposed judgments from God were severe, and David chose the option of three days of plague upon the nation.

This plague was so harsh that in a short time 70,000 people died. But as the angel of the Lord was about to destroy the city of Jerusalem, the calamity was suddenly averted.

How was the harsh tide of judgment turned? What can we learn from David's example in seeking God's mercy and finding a New Beginning of grace?

God's angel tells David to *"build an altar to the LORD on the threshing floor of Ornan the Jebusite"* (v. 18). David obeys this word of instruction, and he tells Ornan: *"Give me the site of this threshing floor, that I may build on it an altar to the LORD; for the **full price** you shall give it to me, that the plague may be restrained from the people"* (v. 22).

Ornan tells David he can have the land for *free*, but the king refuses this generous offer:

No, but I will surely buy it for the full price; for I will not take what is yours for the LORD, or offer a burnt offering which costs me nothing (v. 24).

David's example should be a great lesson for us today. *He refused to give an offering to the Lord that cost him nothing!* True worship always will cost us something! Our offerings are seeds, and unless they're precious to us, they won't be precious to God either. He will never be pleased with our leftovers.

As David gave his sacrificial offering to the Lord, the plague was suddenly stopped: *"The LORD commanded the angel, and he put his sword back in its sheath"* (v. 27).

WHAT PLAGUE ARE YOU FACING?

Are you facing a winter season or "plague" today? Your plague may not be the kind David faced in 1 Chronicles 21, but perhaps it's a broken relationship, an illness, a problem with your children, an addiction, or a financial setback. If you are under some kind of attack like this today, I encourage you to follow David's example and place your sacrificial offering on God's altar!

Many Christians have neglected to honor God with their tithes and with special offerings beyond the minimum 10 percent. Yet the Lord makes it clear that this is the equivalent of *robbing Him*:

"Will a man rob God? Yet you are robbing Me! But you say, 'How have we robbed You?' In tithes and offerings. You are cursed with a curse, for you are robbing Me, the whole nation of you!

"Bring the whole tithe into the storehouse, so that

*there may be food in My house, and test Me now in
this," says the LORD of hosts, "if I will not open for
you the windows of heaven and pour out for you a
blessing until it overflows.*

*"Then I will rebuke the devourer for you, so that it
will not destroy the fruits of the ground; nor will your
vine in the field cast its grapes," says the LORD of
hosts* (Malachi 3:8-11).

This Scripture shows both the positive and negative principles about our financial giving to God:

- When we're disobedient, we are robbing God and *"are
  cursed with a curse."*

- When we faithfully bring God *"the whole tithe,"* He will
  pour out great abundance and rebuke *"the devourer"*—
  the devil who wants to steal, kill, and destroy God's blessings in our lives (John 10:10).

God wants to bless you! He wants to cancel any "plagues"
that have come against your life. And He wants to help you
recapture anything the enemy has stolen from you.

DON'T COME TO GOD EMPTY-HANDED

Often these wonderful benefits of a Covenant
Relationship with the Lord are forfeited when Believers don't
understand God's principles of sowing and reaping...giving
and receiving. God's people miss out on incredible blessings
when they fail to bring Him offerings of their time, their tal-
ent, and their treasure.

When people in Bible days came to worship at the Temple,
they never came without an offering. Whenever they made

their trek to appear before the Lord, they always had a gift in hand that they were bringing as a part of their worship. God instructed them not to appear before Him *"empty-handed"* (Deuteronomy 16:16).

If you've been seeking a New Beginning in an area of your life for a while, but sense that something has been blocking it, I urge you to consider whether you've been robbing God of your financial seeds. The Lord responds to the faith and obedience of His people, and financial faithfulness might be the very key you need to unlock your supernatural breakthrough to a New Beginning!

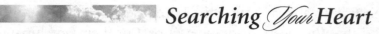 *Searching Your Heart*

1. Describe a time when you honored God by sowing financial seeds in the midst of a "famine" in your life.

2. Have you ever neglected to honor God with your *"firstfruits"* and special offerings? If so, describe that season in your life, recording why you made the choices you did.

3. Write about a winter season or a *"plague"* you may be facing today with a relationship, illness, financial setback, or other difficult circumstance.

4. Spend time now talking with God about your tithes and your offerings.

   ▪ Thank God for His constant faithfulness, His blessings in your life, and every financial seed He has given you to sow.

   ▪ Repent for any ways you have violated His Biblical principle of honoring Him with your tithes and offerings.

   ▪ Ask God for the courage and determination you need to make any changes in your financial giving to His Kingdom. If your finances are a continuing challenge for you, you may need Biblically based financial advice from a Godly friend or counselor. Ask God to show you who you can talk with to get the wisdom, insight, and direction you need, and then make immediate plans to do so.

A NEW BEGINNING OF OBEDIENCE

THE GREAT AMERICAN PREACHER Charles Finney was once asked the secret to experiencing a spiritual revival. Finney replied, "A revival is nothing less than a new beginning of obedience to God."

Take a moment and let Finney's words sink into your heart. Do you want a personal revival of the Lord's presence and blessing in your life? Then here's the secret: You need a New Beginning of obedience to God!

Many Christians assume they're obedient to God simply because they can quote a lot of Bible verses. Yet let's be honest: You could probably train a *parrot* to spout off Bible verses, but that wouldn't mean the parrot is obedient to God!

James addresses this common problem:

> Prove yourselves **doers** of the word, and not merely **hearers** who **delude themselves.** For if anyone is a **hearer** of the word and not a **doer,** he is like a man who looks at his natural face in a mirror; for once he has looked at himself and gone away, he has immediately forgotten what kind of person he was.
>
> But one who looks intently at the perfect law, the law of liberty, and abides by it, not having become a

*forgetful hearer but an **effectual doer**, this man will be **blessed** in what he does* (James 1:22-25).

What a powerful passage of Scripture! It teaches that God's path of blessing is reserved for those who are *doers* of His Word. Those who merely are hearers are *deluding themselves*!

DOERS ARE READY FOR LIFE'S STORMS

The storms of life will come both to Believers and unbelievers. The only question is whether or not we'll have a strong spiritual foundation and be *ready* for these storms of adversity.

Jesus teaches that those who obey His words are prepared for life's storms. Look at the stunning contrast between those who hear and *obey*, and those who merely hear:

*Everyone who hears these words of Mine and acts on them, may be compared to a **wise man** who built his house on the rock. And the rain fell, and the floods came, and the winds blew and slammed against that house; and yet it did not fall, for it had been founded on the rock. Everyone who hears these words of Mine and does not act on them, will be like a **foolish man** who built his house on the sand. The rain fell, and the floods came, and the winds blew and slammed against that house; and it fell—and great was its fall* (Matthew 7:24-27).

Perhaps you're in a storm or winter season already, or perhaps one is on the way. Regardless, your priority must be to serve God with a heart of obedience. Ask Him to reveal any areas of your life that haven't yet been conformed to His Word.

Make sure you've made Jesus the LORD of your life and not just your Savior from sin.

DON'T BE DECEIVED

The pages of Scripture are filled with examples of James' warning about deluding ourselves with the false belief that we are being obedient, when we aren't.

King Saul was told by God,

> *Now go and strike Amalek and **utterly destroy** all that he has, and do not spare him; but put to death both man and woman, child and infant, ox and sheep, camel and donkey* (1 Samuel 15:3).

Although God's command was clear, Saul chose to compromise and rationalize. He *partially* obeyed, but failed to realize this crucial principle: Partial obedience is partial disobedience!

> *He captured Agag the king of the Amalekites alive...**But** Saul and the people spared Agag and the **best** of the sheep, the oxen, the fatlings, the lambs, and all that was good, and were **not willing to destroy them utterly**; but everything **despised** and **worthless**, that they utterly destroyed* (1 Samuel 15:8-9).

Saul obeyed...*BUT*...! Is this the kind of obedience you have toward God today? Do you *partially* obey, but reserve the right to compromise with God's commandment to you?

Saul held back the *best* of what he captured from the Amalekites and only destroyed what was convenient—the livestock that was *"despised and worthless"*!

DON'T RATIONALIZE GOD'S COMMANDS

When the prophet Samuel came to confront King Saul about his disobedience, Saul greeted him with a confident proclamation: *"I have carried out the command of the LORD"* (1 Samuel 15:13).

How sad! Saul seems to have deceived himself into sincerely believing he had obeyed God! But Samuel challenges Saul with the facts: *"What then is this bleating of the sheep in my ears, and the lowing of the oxen which I hear?"* (v. 14) Instead of utterly destroying the Amalekites and their property, as the Lord had commanded, the evidence showed that Saul had intentionally disobeyed.

Even after being confronted with the truth, Saul wasn't done with his rationalizations. He protested that the best of the sheep and oxen had been spared in order to *sacrifice them to the Lord!*

Samuel's reply should be a sobering message to each of us today:

> *Has the LORD as much delight in burnt offerings*
>   *and sacrifices*
> *As in **obeying** the voice of the LORD?*
> *Behold, **to obey is better than sacrifice**,*
> *And to heed than the fat of rams.*
>
> *For rebellion is as the sin of divination,*
> *And insubordination is as iniquity and idolatry.*
> *Because you have rejected the word of the LORD,*
> *He has also rejected you from being king*
>   (1 Samuel 15:22-23).

Don't forget: God is not impressed with religious activity or even sacrifice, unless they are rooted in obedience to His Word and the voice of His Spirit.

THE KEY TO YOUR NEW BEGINNING

Obedience is an indispensable key to your New Beginning. Deuteronomy 28 and other passages describe incredible blessings for those who obey God's voice, as well as curses upon those who disobey.

The Lord sets a clear choice before each of us:

See, I have set before you today life and prosperity, and death and adversity; in that I command you today to love the LORD your God, to walk in His ways and to keep His commandments and His statutes and His judgments, that you may live and multiply, and that the LORD your God may bless you in the land where you are entering to possess it...

I call heaven and earth to witness against you today, that I have set before you life and death, the blessing and the curse. So choose life in order that you may live, you and your descendants, by loving the LORD your God, by obeying His voice, and by holding fast to Him; for this is your life and the length of your days (Deuteronomy 30:15-20).

What choice will you make today? Life or death? The blessing or the curse? By loving and obeying the Lord, you will *"choose life"* and discover God's abundant blessings.

If you truly desire a New Beginning in your life today, ask the Lord to show you any areas of your life where you have rationalized His truth and disobeyed His commandments. Take Charles Finney's advice and commit yourself to a New Beginning of obedience to God!

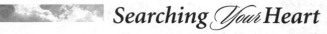 *Searching Your Heart*

1. Read Deuteronomy 28 and Deuteronomy 30:15-20. What do these Scripture passages say about God's blessings for obedience and His curses on disobedience?

2. Make a list of the blessings you've received because of your obedience to God and His Word.

3. Ask Him to reveal through His Holy Spirit any ways you may have rationalized His commands or disobeyed His Word. Make a list of these as well.

4. Spend time now talking with God about your obedience to Him.

   ▪ Thank God for His mercy, which endures *forever*. Worship Him for sending us His Son, Who never disobeyed His Heavenly Father. Praise Him that because Jesus lives inside of you, you can have the desire, courage, and strength to obey your Heavenly Father. Thank Him for the blessings you've received from Him because of your obedience.

   ▪ Next, use the list you made to repent for any of the ways you've rationalized God's commands or disobeyed His Word.

   ▪ Now tell God you want to be a *"doer of the Word and not merely a hearer"* (James 1:22). Ask Him to give you the desire, courage, and strength to obey Him. If you see areas where you need to take action because of past disobedience, make immediate plans with Him to carry out the necessary changes.

WHAT ARE *You* WAITING FOR?

PERHAPS YOU'RE STILL WONDERING if God is truly able to give you the New Beginning you've desired.

I've met many people over the years who hear this message of New Beginnings, but are convinced their situation is just too bleak for God to remedy. They tell me, "David, if you knew what I'm going through, you'd realize it's hopeless—even for God."

In the concluding pages of this book, let me encourage you that God has a track record when it comes to New Beginnings. For thousands of years, He's shown Himself as the *God of New Beginnings*, taking sinful, defeated, and broken people and turning them into new creations. He takes special delight in the "hard cases," intervening in seemingly hopeless situations with breakthroughs only He can provide.

What kind of New Beginning do you need today? No matter what kind of winter season you find yourself in, there's an example of someone in the pages of Scripture who found victory over similar circumstances:

- *If people or geography have held you back from your prophetic destiny in the Lord...*

   Remember Abraham, who at age 75 was called by

God to leave his relatives and the idolatrous culture of Ur in order to venture out to a Promised Land that the Lord had prepared for him and his descendants (Genesis 12:1-4).

■ *If you've been victimized and mistreated, causing you physical or emotional trauma...*

Remember **Joseph**, who forgave his jealous brothers even though they had thrown him into a well and sold him into slavery (Genesis 50:18-21).

Remember the **woman at the well** (John 4:1-42) and the **woman caught in adultery** (John 8:1-11), who both were traumatized at the hands of men and their own foolish choices—yet they each received a New Beginning when Jesus forgave and restored them.

■ *If you've been ridiculed, rejected, or labeled "a pain"...*

Remember **Jabez**, who overcame a difficult childhood by crying out to God for a New Beginning of prosperity and blessing (1 Chronicles 4:9-10).

■ *If you've suffered the grief and pain of losing a loved one...*

Remember **Naomi** and **Ruth**, who found a wonderful New Beginning when they moved back to Judah (Ruth 1:1-22).

■ *If you've committed immorality or an act of violence against another person...*

Remember **David**, who received God's forgiveness and cleansing after committing adultery with Bathsheba and murdering her husband, Uriah (Psalm 51, Psalm 32:1-5).

- *If you're facing insurmountable financial struggles...*

  Remember the **widow at Zarephath**, who found God's supernatural provision when she sacrificially provided for Elijah despite her own need (1 Kings 17:8-16).

- *If you're facing a serious illness...*

  Remember **Naaman**, the Syrian general who was healed of leprosy when he obeyed the prophet Elisha's instructions and dipped seven times in the Jordan River (2 Kings 5:1-27).

  Remember **King Hezekiah**, whose life was extended by years when he seemed to be on his deathbed (2 Kings 20:1-6).

  Remember the **woman with a hemorrhage**, who suffered for 12 years before receiving a supernatural healing when she touched the hem of Jesus' garment (Mark 5:25-34).

- *If you've been bound by fear, depression, or some other form of oppression from the enemy...*

  Remember how Jesus set the **Gerasene demoniac** free from Satan's bondage into glorious liberty (Mark 5:1-20).

- *If you've allowed fear and cowardice to cause you to deny your relationship with the Lord...*

  Remember **Peter**, who denied the Lord three times yet received a New Beginning of leadership in God's Kingdom (John 21:15-17).

- *If you've been religious, but realize you lack an intimate relationship with the Lord...*

Remember **Nicodemus**, who learned that he needed to be born again (John 3:1-8).

Remember **Saul of Tarsus**, who was zealous for religious laws, but was dramatically converted on the road to Damascus (Acts 9:1-19).

- *If you've strayed from God and squandered your life in wild living and addiction…*

Remember the **Prodigal Son**, who found a New Beginning when he made a decision to return to his father's house (Luke 15:11-32).

All these people—and many, many more—received a New Beginning from God. They were just ordinary people who cried out to an extraordinary God.

LEARN FROM THE LEPERS

I need to share one additional story about four men in 2 Kings 7:3-14 who received a New Beginning from God. These men were in a truly desperate situation. They were lepers…they were outcasts…their city was under attack…and they were starving. It wasn't a pretty picture. Hope was nearly gone.

Finally, these lepers got an idea. *"Why should we sit here until we die?"* they asked each other (v. 3). They realized that if they just sat there and did nothing, they would surely die. So they decided to take the risky move of going to the camp of their enemies, the Arameans. *"If they spare us, we will live; and if they kill us, we will but die"* (v. 4).

To the shock of these four lepers, when they reached the camp of the Arameans, they discovered that the camp had been abandoned. Their step of faith—born of desperation—reaped an unbelievable harvest of silver, gold, clothes, and other bounty!

These men would surely have died if they had stayed at the outskirts of the city, grumbling, complaining, blaming others, and full of self-pity for their plight. But they took action—bold action—and received an incredible New Beginning from God.

Friend, sometimes a New Beginning requires a step of faith: a geographical move...the sowing of a financial seed...an act of forgiveness and reconciliation...a season of prayer and fasting. Naaman had to dip seven times in the Jordan, the woman with the hemorrhage had to touch Jesus' cloak, and Job needed to pray for his friends.

Sometimes we're waiting on God to deliver us from some kind of difficult situation, when He's waiting on US to obey the voice of His Spirit and take action! As you pray for God's intervention in your circumstances, make sure you're also listening to His instructions on what you're to *do*.

WHAT'S YOUR NEXT STEP?

As you are sensitive to the voice of God's Spirit, He will show you the steps YOU need to take for your New Beginning. Don't procrastinate. Don't make excuses or blame others for the winter seasons of your life. Don't give up asking God for the breakthrough you need.

You have a Heavenly Father who loves you deeply. He has a fantastic plan for your life (Jeremiah 29:11). He wants to empower you with His Holy Spirit and give you every resource you need for an abundant life in Christ (John 10:10).

God will be faithful to give you a New Beginning today, and He'll also be faithful to *continue* that work of transformation in the days, weeks, months, and years ahead. Remember the wonderful promise:

He who began a good work in you will be
faithful to complete it! – Philippians 1:6

I'm praying that God will meet you at the point of your need today...

Father, may this precious child of Yours be released from their winter season into a New Beginning of obedience, blessing, and abundance. May nothing stand in their way as they pursue Your best for their life! In Jesus' name. Amen.

 ## *Searching Your Heart*

1. Prayerfully reread the list in this chapter of the ordinary people who cried out to an extraordinary God for their New Beginning.

2. Now make your own list of the Biblical characters with whom you most identify. Write down the similarities you see between their situations and the difficult circumstances of your own life.

3. What steps of faith is God showing you to take in order to start your New Beginning *now?* How have rationalizations, excuses, or blame-shifting kept you from taking these steps of faith in the past?

4. Spend time now talking with God about your New Beginning.

   - Worship God as the source of all New Beginnings. Praise Him for His righteousness, faithfulness, love, grace, and mercy in helping you make a New Beginning in *your* life.

   - Repent for any past excuses or blame shifting. Ask God to give you the breakthrough you need to step out in faith and courage to start your New Beginning.

   - Memorize 2 Corinthians 5:17; *"If anyone is in Christ, he is a new creature: old things are passed away; behold, all things have become new."*

   - Repeat this verse to yourself throughout the coming weeks and months as you leave your winter season behind and enter into the springtime of your New Beginning in the Lord!

ABOUT THE AUTHOR

DAVID CERULLO graduated from Oral Roberts University with a degree in Business Administration and Management. After college, David joined his dad to serve at Morris Cerullo World Evangelism and gradually assumed most responsibilities for the day-to-day operations of the ministry. He was ordained for ministry in 1974.

Because of his vision to impact people for Christ worldwide through media, David combined his strong business skills with his passion for souls to assume the leadership of a fledgling Christian cable television network in 1990. With God's help and guidance, David established Inspiration Ministries, an international media ministry that touches lives throughout the world.

David and his wife Barbara have been married for more than 30 years and have two adult children and four grandchildren. David and Barbara host a popular daily television program, "Inspiration Today!"

Visit David and Barbara's website at:

www.inspiration.org

for a current program schedule, a ministry
update, or to request prayer.